PROFITABLE BUYING STRATEGIES

PROFITABLE BUYING STRATEGIES

How to cut procurement costs and buy your way to higher profits

MIKE BUCHANAN

KOGAN
PAGE

London and Philadelphia

First published in Great Britain and the United States in 2008 by Kogan Page Limited

120 Pentonville Road
London N1 9JN
United Kingdom
www.koganpage.com

525 South 4th Street, #241
Philadelphia PA 19147
USA

© Mike Buchanan, 2008

The right of Mike Buchanan to be identified as the author of this work has been asserted by him in accordance with the Copyright, Designs and Patents Act 1988.

ISBN 978 0 7494 5238 4

British Library Cataloguing-in-Publication Data

A CIP record for this book is available from the British Library.

Library of Congress Cataloging-in-Publication Data

Buchanan, Mike, 1957–
   Profitable buying strategies : how to cut procurement costs and buy
your way to higher profits / Mike Buchanan.
      p. cm.
   Includes bibliographical references and index.
   ISBN 978-0-7494-5238-4
1. Purchasing. 2. Industrial procurement. I. Title.
   HF5437.B78 2008
   658.7'2--dc22

                                    2008011172

Typeset by Saxon Graphics Ltd, Derby
Printed and bound in India by Replika Press Pvt Ltd

To Sarah and Kerry, my wonderful daughters,
who never reduced *my* costs

Contents

List of figures

List of tables

List of case studies

Preface and acknowledgements

In my procurement career, I've been reducing costs for employers and clients for many years, and now, in common with many procurement consultants, I routinely save millions of pounds for my clients, every year. In recent years, I've occasionally wondered if I could write a book that captured the essence of my knowledge about cost reduction. And I'm pleased (and more than a little relieved) to say I could – and have.

If you're charged with reducing your organization's costs, this book is for you. It will equip you with all the insights and practical tools you will need to reduce the costs of the goods and services your organization buys. And I've gone to some effort to write it in 'plain English', and keep the jargon out.

Over many years in procurement I've been privileged to work with some very talented professionals, too many to mention here. But I'd like to mention Andrew Heslop, a highly talented fellow consultant, and a good friend. He landed a publishing deal for his own business book in early 2007, while I was still undecided about whether to start writing one myself. Without his constant encouragement from the start, this book would have been neither started nor completed. The book is all the stronger because of the innumerable conversations Andrew and I have had about procurement in general, and cost reduction in particular.

I should like to thank Justin King, chief executive of Sainsbury's, for his agreement that I meet with his senior executives to explore their approaches to cost reduction. The company's David Brooks, Neil Sachdev and Amanda Heffer were particularly helpful, and the result is

Appendix 5. The company also has a great story to relate on corporate responsibility, which is briefly described in Appendix 4.

My warm thanks also to Jon Hughes, Bill Michels and Mark Ralf, for their permission to use materials from their book concerning a major procurement change programme at SmithKline Beecham, credited with saving the company over £200 million in the 1990s. The story is outlined in Appendix 6.

My thanks to David Sheridan, the former Group purchasing and insurance director of Whitbread plc, in my view the author of the best book ever written on negotiating commercial contracts, which I draw upon in a number of places in this book. At 81, he still presents the occasional lecture. He's an inspiration.

My thanks to Alan Bracken of ABTS Logistics, for his permission to use some of his materials on international buying, in Chapter 5.

Finally, I should like to thank my commissioning editor at Kogan Page, Annie Knight, for her professional, enthusiastic and cheerful support at all times. Her colleagues were also a pleasure to work with.

I really enjoyed writing this book. I hope you enjoy reading it, and find it helps you with your noble endeavour to reduce your organization's costs. Good luck!

Introduction

'Where shall I begin, please your Majesty?' he asked. 'Begin at the beginning,' the King said, gravely, 'and go on till you come to the end: then stop.'

(*Lewis Carroll:* Alice's Adventures in Wonderland, *1865*)

The purpose of this book is to enable you to make your organization more profitable. It will therefore be of interest to a broad range of people holding responsibility for improving commercial performance. At least seven 'audiences' will find this book of value:

- senior executives who have been given 'procurement' as part of their range of responsibilities, and need a thorough but fast grounding in the subject;
- executives charged with reducing costs across their organization;
- owner-managers of SMEs (small to medium-sized enterprises) – even relatively modest turnover businesses can improve profitability through better buying;
- people who have been given a procurement role, yet have little experience or formal training in driving out cost,
- people undergoing formal training in procurement, who need a 'real world' explanation of cost reduction options, and 'what works';
- procurement executives who need a fuller understanding of the subject of cost reduction;
- sales and marketing executives who need a deeper understanding of how 'cost reduction experts' approach the task of cost reduction.

Through understanding and applying the principles in this book, you will be able to reduce your organization's costs, boost your career and make a solid business case for improving your remuneration.

Certain parts of the book are necessarily quite 'technical' and 'dry', but I've included numerous anecdotes and 'war stories' which will lighten your reading task, as well as enlighten you. This book will give you all the tools and techniques you need. All you require is the motivation to apply the principles to your specific circumstances.

Please trust me when I tell you that people like myself, whose prime working activity is cost reduction, actually enjoy their work. Reducing costs needn't be a difficult or unpleasant chore – quite the opposite, in fact.

THE BOTTOM LINE

Cost control is important for commercial organizations, because of one simple but inescapable equation:

$$PROFIT = SALES REVENUE - COSTS$$

Organizations that wish to improve their profits have only three options. They can:

- increase sales prices;
- increase sales volumes;
- reduce costs.

For many organizations, in many sectors, competitive pressures are making the first two options increasingly difficult, which leaves cost reduction as a key option to improve profits. And yet the vast majority of organizations do not have long-term, structured approaches to cost reduction. Efforts in many organizations are often limited to a few ad hoc activities, such as vendor switching and price negotiation.

WHY A POUND SAVED IS WORTH MORE THAN A POUND EARNED

Most businesses invest significant resources in achieving revenue growth, yet relatively little effort is expended on a structured approach to reducing costs. The next few paragraphs explain why cost reduction is so important and why it can make an important contribution to the bottom line. To illustrate the point, let's take a manufacturing company with a £100 million pa turnover, and a raw material spend of £50 million pa (the numbers are, of course, quite arbitrary – turnover could be, say, £100,000, £1 million, £1 billion... whatever). Table 0.1 demonstrates the profit improvement impacts of two options, namely increasing sales volumes by 10 per cent, and reducing raw material costs by 10 per cent.

Table 0.1 Comparison between profit improvement options (all figures £m pa)

	Current	Impact of a 10% increase in sales volumes	Impact of a 10% reduction in raw material costs
Turnover	100.0	110.0	100.0
Less:			
Fixed costs	20.0	20.0	20.0
Variable costs:			
Raw materials	60.0	66.0	54.0
Others (inc. labour)	10.0	11.0	10.0
Total costs	90.0	97.0	84.0
PROFIT	10.0	13.0	16.0
PROFIT IMPACT		+30%	+60%

Now it should be clear from this example that while each additional pound earned through sales volume growth will deliver just 30p additional profit, each pound saved by reducing raw material costs flows straight to the bottom line. And the profit impact of the second option is double that of the first.

In practice, however, in most organizations, the improved income stream that flows from cost reduction efforts finances one or more of a number of options:

- increasing capital investment;
- developing a 'war chest' for future acquisitions;
- improving returns to the company owners;
- improving remunerations for key company workers, to help with recruitment and retention;
- enabling selling prices to be reduced, to stimulate sales volumes and thereby grow market share.

PROFESSIONAL COST MANAGEMENT

My objective in writing this book is simple – I want to explain to you, in plain English, how to reduce your organization's costs. That is, I want you to understand what you need to be, to think and to do in order to manage costs professionally.

When you understand and follow some or all of the 10 keys to cost reduction, you will be empowered to achieve results that will surprise and delight you – and your organization. And the more of the keys you use, the more you will reduce your costs. I'm not just talking about the short term here. Professional cost management should be your objective over the long term; it should become 'a way of life'. The day may be coming in your sector – indeed, it may already have arrived – when anything less than a professional approach to cost management will threaten the financial viability of your organization.

Broadly speaking, professional cost management practices have been adopted by industrial sectors in the sequence one might have expected. That is, the higher the proportion of a company's revenues that are spent with third parties, the greater the need to manage the spend professionally. Professional cost management practices have been adopted by sectors in the following sequence:

Sector	% of revenue spent with third parties
Retail	75%+
Manufacturing	50–70%
Services	20–50%

THE 10 KEYS TO COST REDUCTION

Most of my working life has been devoted to reducing costs, and since 1999 I have worked as an independent procurement consultant. I've bought a large number of goods and services, for many organizations, in many sectors, and enjoyed almost every minute of it. I've concentrated most of what I know about the subject of cost reduction into just 10 keys to cost reduction. I've spoken to other procurement consultants whom I regard highly, and they haven't been able to think of any more keys.

Each key is the subject of an individual chapter in this book, as shown in Table 0.2.

Table 0.2 The 10 keys to cost reduction

Keys	Summary
1. The philosophy and psychology of buying	It is crucial to have an appropriate buying philosophy and buying psychology. They underpin all that is to follow.
2. Important buying concepts	A number of buying concepts are provided, to give an 'intellectual base' for cost reduction efforts.
3. Effective tools and techniques	A number of practical tools and techniques are provided, which will help guide the cost reduction effort.
4. The changes that deliver cost reductions	There are only a finite number of change options to reduce costs (change WHAT is bought, change HOW it is bought etc). The options are presented in detail.
5. Market testing	Rigorous market testing lies at the heart of most successful cost reduction drives. This chapter explains the various options available.
6. Outsourcing and insourcing	The corporate activities that are deemed worthy for outsourcing are increasing over time. This chapter provides insights into the different types of outsourcing, and a detailed section on legal issues to be considered.
7. Negotiation	Negotiation is one of a number of available approaches to reduce cost, but not necessarily a very important one. This is explained, along with advice on how to improve your negotiating competence.
8. Contracts and contract law	All too many cost reduction drives are compromised by poorly drafted contracts, of inappropriate durations. This chapter tackles this important area.
9. E-procurement	E-procurement is an increasingly important cost reduction tool for organizations, and most organizations have spend areas that are suitable for its application. This chapter gives insights into this area, and will help you decide which of your spend areas might be suited to the approach.
10. Organizational issues	Numerous organizational issues are important in the context of cost reduction efforts, and they are covered here.

As well as the 10 chapters on the keys to cost reduction, I've provided seven appendices, which will be of varying levels of relevance and interest to individual readers:

1.   Service level agreement (SLA);
2.   Request for proposal (RFP);
3.   Chartered Institute of Purchasing and Supply;
4.   Soft issues impacting on cost reduction drives;
5.   Buying at Sainsbury's supermarkets;
6.   Buying at SmithKline Beecham;
7.   Buyer remuneration in the UK.

It just remains for me to wish you well with your cost reduction efforts. I hope this book both informs and inspires you.

A BRIEF NOTE ON TERMINOLOGY

You may be excused any confusion you have over terms such as 'buying', 'purchasing' and 'procurement'. The terms largely reflect job title inflation over the years – in the same way that 'Personnel' has become 'Human Resources', and 'Sales' has become 'Account Management' or 'Company Development'. For the purpose of this book, I'll use the three terms 'buying', 'purchasing' and 'procurement' interchangeably, as befits the context at that point.

1

The philosophy and psychology of buying

The reasonable man adapts himself to the world: an unreasonable one persists in trying to adapt the world to himself. Therefore all progress depends on the unreasonable man.

(George Bernard Shaw: Man and Superman, *1903)*

This chapter contains:

- The philosophy of buying.
- The psychology of buying.
- Vendor conditioning of buyers.
- Personality types and aptitudes.
- Risk management.

THE PHILOSOPHY OF BUYING

In many professions, a number of books are considered to have enormous merit long after they have been published. David Sheridan's *Negotiating Commercial Contracts*, published in 1991, is such a book.

Sheridan was the Group purchasing and insurance director of Whitbread and Company plc until 1986, and was then, and later, an internationally renowned speaker and writer on buying, negotiation and related topics. The book is sadly out of print, but 'as new' copies are currently available on Amazon and elsewhere, at bargain prices. Buy a copy if you can. It's a great read.

The book is full of insights and valuable advice, and Sheridan's clarity of thought on complex matters is refreshing, drawing on his deep well of experience. I have included some brief sections of the book later on. But for the purpose of this section, it's Sheridan's 'buying philosophy' that I'd like to commend to you.

Sheridan's buying philosophy was simple, and summarized by one sentence in the book: 'Negotiating decisions should be made on the basis of business strategy, and what will produce the best short-, medium- or long-term effects, depending on the nature of the goods or services to be sold, or acquired.'

Nothing there about reaching 'amicable compromises' with vendors, nor 'loyalty' towards them, nor any of the innumerable 'softer issues' that buyers are sometimes exhorted to consider, at the expense of the best contract(s) they can negotiate.

Most successful buying consultants have a buying philosophy much like Sheridan's. The reason is simple. The philosophy leads to savings of millions of pounds a year for their clients. Sheridan is now 81, and still lectures occasionally. That must tell you something of the power of a robust 'buying philosophy'.

Whatever one may think about 'softer issues' such as corporate social responsibility, sustainable procurement, and the rest, there is no doubt that they tend to add unhelpful confusion to the search for cost reduction, whatever their proponents might claim. Now, attention to such issues might be required as part of a company's 'business philosophy', for example if the company is in the public eye, such as a major retailer. But the vast majority of commercial organizations simply aren't in the public eye to any significant degree.

It seems to me that too many professional buyers are strongly motivated by 'soft issues', at the expense of their duty to minimize costs for their companies. The truth is that many of them are temperamentally unsuited to the 'trading role' of which Sheridan writes. It follows that they are spending more money than they should for goods and services, in pursuit of 'soft issues'. Are their employers aware of this fact, let alone the extent of the extra spend? Appendix 4 covers the issue of soft issues.

THE PSYCHOLOGY OF BUYING

Large sums of money are spent by organizations on goods and services, and the financial implications of buying either poorly or well are substantial. You might reasonably expect there to be a large body of academic research on the psychology of buying – but you'd be wrong. Academic interest appears largely confined to the psychology of negotiating, which is only one element of buying.

For over 20 years, I've observed how people behave in real commercial situations, and I've explored their thinking in some detail, which I term the 'psychology of buying'. This chapter summarizes my experience of the psychology of buying, and numerous successful buyers have told me it aligns closely with their own experiences.

Motivation

In our work-related roles, as in our personal lives, motivation is a key issue. Of all the different objectives we might seek to realize, and choices over how we spend our limited time, what will we do? For most buyers this is the easy part, because cost reduction is invariably one of their key objectives.

Buyers will be motivated by one or more of a range of possible outcomes, should they be successful in their efforts:

- monetary reward, possibly higher income or a bonus;
- promotion;
- the appreciation of the organization;
- raised self-esteem from 'a job well done';
- continued employment.

Now non-buyers are rarely motivated in the same manner, however large the budgets for which they are responsible. Budgets tend to reflect historical actual costs, rather than costs currently obtainable in the marketplace. Many organizations still hold to the questionable practice of increasing budget lines by the general rate of inflation every year, so a large gap can – and often does – appear between budget prices and marketplace prices over time. But without proficient market testing, the gap may not be discovered, and non-buyers can satisfy their organizations simply by meeting budgets. They are not motivated to reduce costs. Find out what will motivate them to market test, eg a bonus of x per cent of savings delivered, and watch the outcome.

Beliefs and attitudes

I have worked with a considerable number of people engaged in buying. For some of these people ('buyers'), buying is their prime activity, while for many ('non-buyers') it is not, the latter generally having senior budget-holding responsibilities in Finance, HR, Operations, IT, Facilities etc. It's worth pointing out that while the latter group will not have the term 'buyer' – or something equivalent – within their job title, they may still in fact spend a good deal of their working life on buying activities.

It has become clear to me that successful buyers and non-buyers share a set of beliefs and attitudes which together constitute a 'commercial mindset'. To a detached observer they will appear highly 'unreasonable' in a buying scenario – particularly during negotiations – but we shall see in Chapter 7 why unreasonableness is so important, indeed vital.

Successful buyers are NOT reasonable, as this term is commonly used. They don't 'split the difference' in negotiations, and they don't see themselves as responsible for the happiness of salespersons. And they are not 'loyal' to vendors, in the loose way in which the term is often used. Sheridan has some good points to make about loyalty:

> One of the most overworked words in the buyer's and seller's vocabulary, 'loyalty', is also one of the most misused. Sellers invoke it when expecting a customer to stay with them, despite competitors' more attractive offers. Buyers use it when urging suppliers to give them preferential treatment in periods of short supply. 'Haven't we stayed with you over all these years?' goes the cry. 'There's no loyalty left, it seems, in today's climate.' 'Loyalty' is defined as the process of being 'faithful', 'firm in allegiance', 'personally devoted' – characteristics one would hardly expect to apply to transactions of a commercial or financial nature.
>
> Successful negotiators give no credence to loyalty in their deliberations, certainly not in the way it is usually described. More important is an adherence to their bargains, whether they turn out to be as profitable as expected or not, a tough, but even-handed, approach to all suppliers or customers and a climate in which 'favours' are neither expected nor proffered. In the loose way the term 'loyalty' is used in most businesses, it is hardly surprising that buyers and sellers use it as a weapon with which to get their own way.

It is clear that there are many people who do not have a commercial mindset, and such people should have as little responsibility for buying as possible. In our private lives we live in a world of generally fixed prices, and can find infrequent negotiations for big-ticket items (houses/cars) stressful. But in a corporate role we're PAID to feel uncomfortable at times.

People can be averse to confrontation in their personal lives, while happily embracing confrontation as buyers. And confrontation doesn't necessarily entail aggression. The most successful negotiators I know are very rarely – if ever – aggressive with vendors; they simply and calmly explain to the vendors what will follow if they fail to improve their offers – usually loss of business to better value for money competitors.

My company delivers workshops on 'Commercial Awareness' and 'Commercial Negotiation'. Most delegates on these courses (generally non-buyers) come away highly motivated, and keen to apply the tools and techniques they've learnt. They take pleasure in telling us weeks or months – even years – later that they've saved £80,000 on this, £200,000 on that…

But we are sometimes reminded of the limitations of training. At one client, an executive (a man) was clearly highly uncomfortable with negotiating, and another executive (a woman) beat him very convincingly in a negotiation role-play exercise. He played the part of a man who wanted to sell a car for at least £1,000, she played the part of a buyer who did not want to spend more than £800. In the end she negotiated the price down to £700.

The first executive claimed to have learnt a lot from the exercise, but a week later I uncovered an area where a vendor had been overcharging for years. The executive's response haunts me to this day: 'Do you think they'd mind awfully if we asked them for a small price reduction, going forward? Let bygones be bygones!' Some people are simply beyond help. No amount of training could have turned this man into a competent buyer.

All this raises the question of the extent to which people can learn a commercial attitude. My experience is that most people can, but not everyone wants to.

Unhelpful mindsets

There are numerous remarks made by people who do not have a commercial mindset. The following is but a small selection of such remarks, my 'top ten'.

1. 'Our buyers are meeting their budgets, so they're buying proficiently.'

Budgets are a notoriously poor way to measure buying performance. It may sound obvious, but it's often forgotten that budgets are usually set with historical costs in mind, not costs currently obtainable in the marketplace. If you were to buy a new car for personal use, would you look at the price of new cars three years ago, apply the rate of inflation in the intervening period, and set out to spend exactly that sum? Of course not. You would see what was currently available, at what price. You would 'market test'.

One of our professional services clients had two offices in a city in the north of England, each of which had contracts with different vendors for archiving (the storage and retrieval of documents). One had been paying over twice the costs of the other for the same services, with a different vendor, for many years. We looked into the matter, and soon discovered that the higher-paying office enjoyed a much higher budget, resulting from historical costs, and that the two offices had never compared pricing with one another in this area, or indeed any other areas.

2. 'We have a buyer, so we're proficient at buying.'

But how effective IS your buyer? After all, 50 per cent of buyers perform at below average levels. Without assessment by an external expert, you can't know how effective your buyer is, because you have no way of tracking how they perform, compared to similar people in other organizations. On a number of occasions I've started working for a new client, and it's quickly become obvious to me that the performance of one or more of the buyers is dire. Very often, this comes as a complete surprise to the senior managers in the organization – 'Harry has been doing that job for over 20 years, we thought he was good at it!'

All performance is relative. I sometimes ask attendees the following question in negotiation workshops: 'Hold a hand up if, in a given set of circumstances, your negotiation outcome would be superior to that achieved by the average buyer.' It may not surprise you to learn that in every workshop I've held, everyone raised a hand. When I asked if they agreed that half of them must be wrong, they fully agreed – but cheerfully continued asserting their personal superiority. It seems to be a part of human nature to flatter oneself on one's abilities, when there's no obvious external benchmark.

I find that even the most competent buyers and non-buyers can get slowly worn down by vendors over time, and become more and more conditioned by them – and they thereby become less challenging than they should be, whether in the area of price or elsewhere. This is the thinking behind the periodic changes of responsibilities of some buyers in major organizations – a number of them are famous for it.

3. 'You get what you pay for.'

This roughly means 'quality is proportional to price', so if you negotiate lower prices, quality will suffer. The idea is perfectly captured in an old saying, which has frequently been put to me by vendors desperately trying to persuade me to buy from them, rather than from a less expensive competitor: 'The bitterness of poor quality is tasted long after the sweetness of a low price is forgotten.'

But quality – in the sense of consistency with specification – will be governed by the contract, so the lower-cost vendor will still have to deliver to requirements.

I regularly see this mindset with regard to copier paper, where people routinely expect lower-price paper to lead to more copier jams. But let's say you're currently buying copier paper at £4.00/ream, with the specification outlined in Table 1.1. If you negotiate a lower price for the same paper, say £2.00/ream, will you suffer more copier jams? Of course not. We'll return to the important topic of specifications in Chapter 3.

Table 1.1   Basic specification for copier paper

Characteristics	Test methods	Values	Tolerances
Substance	ISO 536	80 gsm	±0.5 gsm
Thickness	ISO 534	104 microns	±3 microns
Surface roughness	ISO 8791–2	233 ml/min	±2 ml/min
Whiteness	ISO 11475	142	±4
Opacity	ISO 2471	90%	±2%

4. 'Our vendor is on a razor-thin margin on this one.'

I recently had a meeting with a client's IT executive, who was asking for my sign-off on a five-year IT project, for which a budget of £1 million had been approved. He said he hadn't revealed the budget to any of the three potential vendors, but all had pitched their initial proposals at around £1.20–1.30m. He had negotiated with them until one was willing to sign the contract for £1.01m.

It became clear in the course of our discussion that he had simply stopped negotiating once the vendor was very close to the budgeted figure. When I asked for the reason, he explained that the vendor was on 'a razor-thin margin', and couldn't drop his price any further.

When I asked him how he knew the margin was very thin, he responded with a plaintive 'because the salesperson said it was'. He had absolutely no independent evidence for the size of the vendor's margin, but this clearly didn't trouble him. He was truly shocked when I suggested the salesperson might have lied.

A related mindset is often expressed as 'our vendors need to make a decent profit to survive'. But buyers are paid to support the profitability of their own organizations, not that of their vendors. In most cases, individual customers will have a small impact on a vendor's overall profitability, unless they buy a substantial proportion of that vendor's output. In which case they will clearly need to address the risk that the vendor may cease to trade if their profitability is inadequate, thereby damaging the buyer's business. Developing other sources, if possible, may be worth considering.

As a leading procurement consultant, Andrew Heslop once pointed out, 'there's no budget line termed altruism'. If buyers wish to pay more than they need to, they should get their firms' owners' prior agreement to the charitable approach.

5. 'I've been buying this service for 20 years, and our terms are very competitive.'

While there are exceptions, executives who make such comments can usually be relied upon to have one year's experience, 20 times over. It may be counter-intuitive to the reader, but professional buyers know that they can generally save more money in a spend area previously managed by an individual for 20 years than in one previously managed by an individual for two years. They bring a fresh eye and plenty of energy to the challenge.

6. 'We're not buying widgets, you know!'

Lines of this nature tend to be used by executives who believe that professional buying approaches may be suitable for buying some simple goods and services, but not for their specialist areas. They are invariably wrong.

7. 'We already get very high discounts from our vendors.'

What matters is the price paid, not the discount that leads to it. A focus on discounts, while ignoring (possibly unseen) base price list increases, is a strong indicator of poor buying thinking. Let's consider a scenario where vendor X is offering you a 10 per cent discount from their price list, while vendor Y is offering you a 50 per cent discount from their price list. If you don't have the base price lists to review, the discount levels in themselves tell you nothing about the relative price competitiveness of the two offerings.

8. 'We're seeking 10 per cent cost reductions in all areas.'

Many executives have a cost reduction 'expectation ceiling' of 10 per cent, and we've even heard some executives say that to seek more would be embarrassing. The reality is that an expertly executed programme will deliver a wide variation of savings from different spend areas, for reasons outlined in later chapters. If you have a low 'expectation ceiling', such as 10 per cent, the overall outcome will clearly be sub-optimal, and certainly far short of 10 per cent. My strong advice is not to have expectation ceilings, as they just stifle ambition. The issue of cost savings potential in different spend areas is covered in Chapters 2 and 3.

9. 'We get professional advice in this area, and pay nothing for it.'

'Free advisers', often termed 'brokers', are common in a few spend areas, notably utilities – at least when market prices are falling. The advisers sometimes share delivered cost savings, but also sometimes receive undisclosed commissions from vendors, the latter being a clear conflict of interest. The issue of markets in which it is difficult to market test is covered in Chapter 5.

10. 'The Christmas bottle of malt whisky is to thank me for past business, not influence future business.'

My heart sinks when I hear this one, or similar lines to justify the acceptance of gifts or hospitality. I'm reminded of the story of a judge in Sicily, who oversaw trials of suspected Mafia members. He was charged with accepting bribes from the Mafia. His defence was that the money was to thank him for past judgements on Mafia members, not to influence future judgements.

VENDOR CONDITIONING OF BUYERS

The term 'conditioning' refers to the efforts made by vendors to change how buyers would otherwise think and feel about:

- the market they're sourcing from;
- them as a vendor;
- them as an individual salesperson.

A lot of this is to do with the vendors' desire to persuade buyers that they should be 'loyal' towards the vendor, for example buyers might:

- market test less frequently than they otherwise would;
- decline to switch to another vendor, unless the case is overwhelming;
- tip them off that a price reduction of x% would help them retain the business;
- be less determined to negotiate as strongly as they otherwise might;
- excuse lapses of quality or performance.

There are a number of ways the salesperson can attain such undue influence. They include:

- Entertainment – I never cease to be amazed by buyers who happily accept invitations to top sports events, expensive restaurants etc, and view themselves as not being influenced. Such lack of self-awareness is a serious flaw in a buyer.
- Friendship – some buyers come to regard their salespeople as friends over time, maybe not realizing that you can't have a robust commercial relationship with a friend.
- Gifts – in workshops I ask buyers how they'd feel if they opened a Christmas card from a vendor and a crisp £50 note fell out. All say they'd be horrified, this would be clearly 'over the line'. Things become less clear-cut when I ask how they'd feel about being given a very good bottle of malt whisky (worth £50) at Christmas. About half see no problem with that. To my mind, the two scenarios are equally unacceptable.

I generally recommend to clients that, as a matter of policy, they forbid staff – within their buying department, and outside it – who deal in any capacity with vendors, to accept any entertainment, lavish meals, or gifts from them. CIPS's Professional Code of Ethics is provided in Appendix 3.

PERSONALITY TYPES AND APTITUDES

There are deeply entrenched views, among many people, about the characteristics of successful salespeople. They say that successful salespeople are generally:

- energetic, extrovert;
- talkers rather than listeners;

- motivated by money and prestige, such as the latest executive car;
- not detail-oriented.

Herein lies a conundrum, because many people also say that some of these characteristics are the very ones that make salespeople annoying to them. How might we explain this?

In both their business and personal lives, few people are called upon to 'sell'. The process of selling tends to be the preserve of dedicated individuals in a sales function, whatever its actual name. As such, people could be forgiven for coming to the view that salespeople are somehow different from them, in a fundamental way.

Buying is different. While not many people buy goods and services for organizations, all of us buy goods and services for ourselves in our personal lives. And if we make a bit of an effort, and steel ourselves to negotiate, we might have had some memorable examples of success, so we see ourselves as 'successful buyers'.

But buying for organizations is different in so many ways. I've often heard it said that organizations would save money if their executives treated the organization's money with the same care as they do their own. Given the level of financial competence demonstrated by so many people, I beg to differ.

As far as reasonably possible, efforts should be made to align the buying of individual spend areas with buyers who have the personality types and aptitudes suited to the task. So one buyer may have a personality and aptitudes suited to negotiating multi-year contracts, in areas with few viable vendors, and where personal relationships have to be developed over time. Another buyer may have a personality and aptitudes suited to negotiating a contract for spend areas with many viable vendors, in a market with relentless overcapacity, and there is no need to develop personal relationships.

RISK MANAGEMENT

You may find it odd to find this subject in a chapter on 'the philosophy and psychology of buying'. But there's a good reason to put it here.

We see in our everyday lives that people exhibit a broad range of attitudes towards risk. Some actively seek it out – people who enjoy dangerous sports perhaps being an obvious example – while some are highly risk-averse, probably in both their personal and working lives.

Risk-averse people will, as one might expect, see a range of risks in cost reduction efforts, which will disincline them to make such efforts. But commercial organizations need to consider two pressing realities here.

1. You will increasingly have no option but to reduce costs

Over time, professional procurement practices are being adopted by ever-smaller organizations. No longer are they the preserve of multinational corporations. If your competitors aren't making serious attempts to reduce their costs, you don't have a problem – although you will still be missing a golden opportunity to improve your profitability.

But if your competitors are making serious attempts to reduce their costs, you have a problem – because their reduced costs will enable them to reduce their selling prices, and thereby gain market share over time. And you simply won't be able to command the price levels that you've enjoyed historically for the goods or services you sell.

2. Cost reduction efforts will lead to some risks, but they're all perfectly manageable

Now I know this to be true, after many years of reducing costs for employers and clients, but why should you take my word for it? Maybe the best I can offer you is an outline of the potential risks that I find trouble most executives, and my responses to them, as outlined in Table 1.2.

I'll leave the final word on risk to a leading procurement executive: 'Any executive in the private sector who wishes to avoid risk, rather than manage it, is working in the wrong sector'(David Oxland, global procurement director, Baxi plc).

Table 1.2   Commonly perceived risks from cost reduction efforts

Risk	Response
The quality of the good/service may be reduced.	If you've set an appropriate specification (Chapter 3) and it's enshrined in your contract (Chapter 8), this will not happen. For goods sourced from overseas, you might use the services of a Pre Shipment Inspection company (Chapter 5). Below-specification goods or services are no more likely from your new vendor than from your incumbent vendor. Indeed they are arguably even less likely, because you might 'excuse' your incumbent vendor, while you wouldn't 'excuse' a new one.
Exchange rates may move adversely.	Exchange rates are as likely to move favourably as adversely, at any point in time. A straightforward mechanism enshrined in the contract will remove some of the risk (Chapter 4), and lead to lower prices in the event of favourable movements. And if the exchange rate moves sufficiently against you, you will be in a position to terminate the contract.
Raw material costs may move adversely.	Raw material costs are as likely to move favourably as adversely, at any point in time. A straightforward mechanism enshrined in the contract will remove some of the risk (Chapter 4), and lead to lower prices in the event of favourable movements. And if raw material costs move sufficiently against you, you will be in a position to terminate the contract.
Delivery of goods may be delayed.	This fear normally arises from consideration of the distance from overseas vendors, maybe on the other side of the world. You simply need to build in a reasonable 'time buffer' to insure against this risk.
My vendors may not be happy at having to supply goods and services at lower prices.	Are you paid to obtain best value for money for your employer, or to make your vendors happy? The vendors will soon recover the money from 'softer' buyers working for other customers.

continued

Table 1.2   *Continued*

Risk	Response
I may be contractually tied to one vendor, when another vendor offers me either an innovation of which I want to take advantage, or substantially lower prices.	Both scenarios are covered in Chapter 8. You would be in a position to terminate the contract in the event of either of these scenarios actually happening.
The new vendor may fail financially, and cease to trade.	Given that checking on potential vendor financial viability is a part of stage 4 in the buying cycle (Chapter 3), it may be less likely that a new vendor will fail financially than your current vendor.

2

Important buying-related concepts

Man... grows beyond his work, walks up the stairs of his concepts, and emerges ahead of his accomplishments

(John Steinbeck: The Grapes of Wrath, *1939)*

This chapter contains:

- Terminology – cost reduction, cost containment, cost avoidance.
- The buying portfolio.
- The Pareto Principle (the '80/20 rule').
- Single sourcing and multi-sourcing.
- Buying power and intrinsic cost reduction potential.
- Market segregation.
- Quality.
- Total cost of ownership (TCO).

In common with many professional buyers, especially those who have bought a broad range of goods and services in a number of sectors, I have come to realize that a fairly limited selection of concepts underpin successful cost reduction initiatives. This chapter will explain those concepts.

TERMINOLOGY – COST REDUCTION, COST CONTAINMENT, COST AVOIDANCE

I commonly find some confusion over the meaning of these terms among non-buyers, so definitions might be useful. For the sake of illustration, let's take a scenario where a buyer sources their printed materials from printer x, and spends £1 million pa with the printer. A number of events might then take place, which can variously be described as cost reduction, cost containment or cost avoidance.

Cost reduction

The buyer moves their business to printer y, and anticipates saving £200,000 pa as a result. Their 'cost reduction' is then £200,000 pa.

Cost containment

The printer seeks a 10 per cent price increase (£100,000 pa) across all items, purportedly to compensate them for rising costs, in areas such as:

- raw materials – papers, inks, varnishes…;
- staff wages;
- rent and rates;
- utilities.

Now if the buyer negotiates with the printer and reduces the increase to 5 per cent, they are said to have negotiated a 'cost containment' of £50,000 pa.

In the old days of high inflation levels, buyers spent a good deal of time on cost containment. In these days of low inflation levels, buyers should be spending little time on it. Any vendor seeking price increases to cover for inflationary pressures should be told that a market testing exercise will be undertaken, unless the price increase proposal is withdrawn. Let other organizations, with 'softer buyers' than you, pay the increases.

The principle can be taken even further. I once heard of a company that told all its vendors that an application for a price increase on any grounds whatsoever would automatically result in a market-testing exercise being undertaken, and under no circumstances would the original vendor be reappointed. The company's rationale was that even if from time to time it had to pay higher prices as a result of the policy, it was more than compensated for by the fact that vendors genuinely had to get to the point that the business was not profitable enough to carry on before they approached the buyer and effectively 'resigned the account'.

Cost avoidance

The buyer realizes that their company can communicate with a range of customers quite adequately electronically, which means they can reduce the value of printed materials they buy by 25 per cent. The saving of £250,000 pa is a 'cost avoidance'.

THE BUYING PORTFOLIO

A seminal paper (Kraljic, 1983) written by a director of the Düsseldorf office of McKinsey, the consulting firm, introduced this concept to the wider world. A great deal of work by buyers and academics has been focused on the concept in the intervening years, and I recommend that readers obtain a copy. A modified version of the concept has been presented to buyers for many years, usually something similar to Figure 2.1. Buyers have been taught that they should place individual spend areas within one of the four quadrants of a matrix, see Figure 2.1.

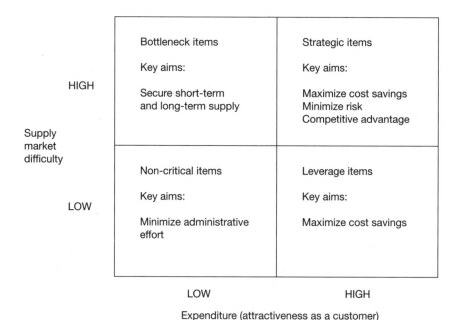

Figure 2.1   *The buying portfolio*

The 'expenditure' axis is self-explanatory, but what about 'supply market difficulty'? Table 2.1 explains.

Table 2.1   Supply market difficulty

Parameter	Supply market difficulty	
	Easy	**Difficult**
Number of vendors with adequate spare capacity	Many	One or a few
Challenge to find viable new vendors	Low	Moderate to high
Effort involved in switching vendors	Low	Moderate to high

Taking each of the four quadrants in turn:

1. Leverage. This is where most of your prime cost reduction opportunities will lie, simply because you're a significant buyer of the goods or services, and there are plenty of viable vendors.
2. Strategic. A difficult area, mainly because there are just one or a few vendors. Your focus should be to work over the long term with one or two vendors, and aim to gain some competitive advantage as a result.
3. Acquisition. While the supply market is not difficult, spend is low, so the emphasis should be on seeking to improve efficiency in this area, and not spend too much time on it. But there may be interesting cost reduction opportunities in this quadrant. I find that most non-buyers place office stationery in this quadrant, but given that a 30%+ cost reduction opportunity often lies in this area, it is almost always worth market testing.
4. Critical. Some engineering spares provide a good example. A spare might cost £5, but if the absence of it might cause a production line to come to a halt, possibly costing a lot of money through lost production, it would obviously be sensible to have a number of such spares, particularly if the item were bespoke and not readily available.

So the buying portfolio is a good way to review a company's spend areas, with a view to determining 'top-level approaches' for each area.

THE PARETO PRINCIPLE (THE '80/20 RULE')

Pareto was an Italian-American who discovered, in the 19th century, a correlation (the 'Pareto Principle') that appears to have wide applicability. His key observation was that in developed countries, around 80 per cent of the country's wealth – in private ownership – was owned by 20 per cent of the population. For many years buyers have been introduced to the principle at an early stage in their training. The key point, in the context of cost reduction, is that some categories are much more important than others.

A commonly quoted example is that of lists of bought items. Let's say you have a list of the items of stationery your company has bought in the past year, in descending spend order. You might well find that the top 20 per cent of items account for approximately 80 per cent of the overall expenditure.

The principle is also applicable to all of your company's spend, and if you were to plot your company's cumulative spend against its cumulative number of goods and services, you might well arrive at a graph similar to Figure 2.2.

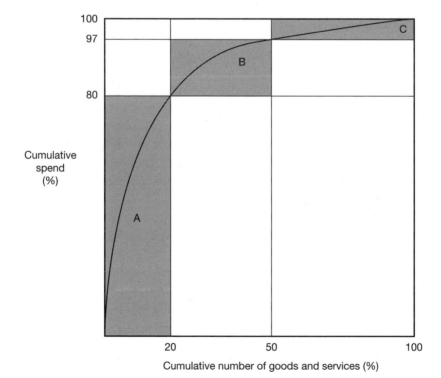

Figure 2.2 *Purchasing and the Pareto curve*

From the figure, we see that:

- 'A-class' spend areas represent 80 per cent of the company's expenditure, but only 20 per cent of its spend areas;
- 'B-class' spend areas represent 17 per cent of expenditure, and 30 per cent of spend areas;
- 'C-class' spend areas represent just 3 per cent of expenditure, but 50 per cent of spend areas.

Some obvious conclusions may be drawn from the analysis, and for the purpose of cost savings, the main conclusion is that most cost reduction potential must be found within A-class spend areas, and possibly a few within B-class spend areas.

Now one obvious question that follows from this is: what proportion of your company's 'A-class' spend areas are subject to ongoing and rigorous procurement attention?

An obvious practical use for the Pareto Principle is effort prioritization. All else being equal, you'd make an effort to reduce the costs of spend areas at the upper end of the list, rather than at the lower end of the list – because the potential cost savings should be higher.

But we must recognize the law of diminishing returns. In many companies, some effort will have been expended, over some years, on reducing the costs associated with the upper spend areas in such tables. It may be, therefore – depending on the effort and expertise applied – that limited cost savings are to be found in these areas. Conversely, some sizeable cost reduction opportunities may lie further down these tables, in 'virgin territory'. I rarely conduct a cost reduction assignment without delivering sizeable cost savings in one or more areas which my client had considered unworthy of attention. That's largely due to my applying my knowledge of intrinsic cost reduction potential within a range of spend areas, a subject which will be explained later in this chapter.

SINGLE SOURCING AND MULTI-SOURCING

Buyers over recent years have become increasingly comfortable with awarding contracts for a spend area to just one vendor ('single sourcing') rather than to two or more vendors ('dual sourcing' or 'multi-sourcing'). But in reality a range of advantages may be cited for each approach. Each spend area needs to be considered on its own merits:

- Advantages of single sourcing to buyers:

- vendors can reflect their improved economies of scale in lower pricing;
- buyers' administrative task is minimized;
- personal relationships are improved, as more time is available to develop them;
- vendors are more likely to make greater efforts to improve quality and delivery timeliness;
- vendors are more likely to undertake research for the buyer, or to give the buyer early access to innovations.
- Advantages of multi-sourcing to buyers:
  - 'competitive tension' will mean that none of the vendors can afford to become complacent;
  - possibility of speedier response to unexpectedly large requirements;
  - reduces the risk of supply discontinuity that might result from industrial action, quality problems, fire etc affecting one vendor;
  - less likely to lead to over-dependence of vendors on an individual customer, which can happen if a large proportion of a vendor's production is devoted to a small number of customers;
  - buyers have more sources of new ideas or materials.

BUYING POWER AND INTRINSIC COST REDUCTION

All else being equal, in most markets, as your demand increases, so does your buying power, or 'leverage', so the more attractive to vendors you will become as a potential customer. Competition among vendors should then lead to lower price offerings.

But that's only part of the story. I am always interested to understand clients' perceptions with regard to cost savings. I sometimes ask them to illustrate graphically how they think the price of a good or service might relate to their company's demand for it. Common sense generally leads them to something like Figure 2.3. That is, they recognize that prices should fall with demand, but there's obviously a limit to how far vendors are prepared to reduce their prices, regardless of order sizes. Very often it does not occur to these executives that the nature of different spend areas might play a part in the relationship between demand and price.

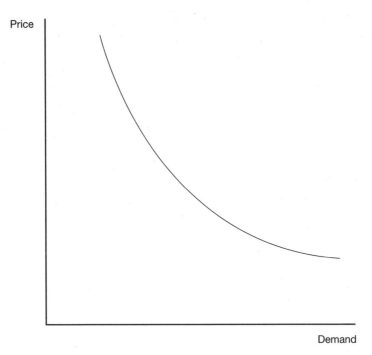

Figure 2.3   *'Common sense' relationship between price and demand*

Then I ask the executives to consider how prices might vary with demand, in a number of specific spend areas, which might include:

- company vehicles;
- utilities, eg electricity;
- mobile phone call charges;
- agency labour;
- printed materials.

At this point, the penny generally drops. Their experience tells them that prices in some spend areas are highly sensitive to demand, while in others they're not. Mobile phone call charges are a good example of the former, agency labour a good example of the latter.

I then go on to ask them why they think this 'price sensitivity' varies so much between different spend areas, and it usually doesn't take them long to work it out. It's all to do with the vendors' internal economics of providing the good or service to new customers.

Let's consider two spend areas with very different price sensitivities.

Cost structure 1 – 'sunk costs' are a high proportion of the selling price

Imagine that your company owns and operates a mobile phone network. When a potential business customer contacts you, possibly operating hundreds or even thousands of mobile phones, you know that he has a choice of a number of networks, of a quality sufficient for his needs. Now for all intents and purposes, almost all your costs are 'sunk costs', in the sense that the cost of building the network, maintaining it, marketing the network, operating the stores, and almost all other costs are sunk costs.

It will cost you very little to provide the potential customer with access to your network, and associated marginal administration and selling costs will be small. So you will be willing and able to drop prices well below those you'd be prepared to make available to private individuals, whose individual demands will be so much smaller than the aggregated demands of a corporate customer. The other network providers are in a similar situation, so the business customer will enjoy the benefits of a fiercely competitive market, and enjoy prices very considerably below those made available to private individuals.

Professional buyers look for spend areas with cost structures of this type, for they are areas of intrinsically high cost reduction potential.

Cost structure 2 – 'sunk costs' are a low proportion of the selling price

Now imagine that your company is an agency supplying temporary office staff. Let's say at a particular client's location, it would cost the client around £10.00/hr to employ a worker with the competences to carry out a particular role. Let's also say the client chooses to source such individuals through agencies such as your own, at a premium over the 'employee rate', for a number of reasons.

You will clearly need to charge your client a commission, to pay for your services. A competitive market for agency labour in the client's area may mean that the average commission obtainable is £2.00/hr, so the client pays a total of £12.00/hr.

The client may seek to reduce their costs in this area, but they face the reality that of the £12.00/hr, £10.00/hr is non-negotiable, in the sense that it's the local market rate for such an individual as an employee. So they can only seek to reduce the £2.00/hr commission.

Professional buyers tend to avoid spend areas with cost structures of this type, for they are areas of intrinsically low cost reduction potential.

In Chapter 3, I'll introduce a technique to help you make a prediction of cost reduction potential within individual spend areas.

MARKET SEGREGATION

We need to consider market segregation at this point. We talk of markets, but there may be several – possibly many – sub-markets. For example, there is little to be gained by thinking of 'the car market'. There are sub-markets for prestigious saloons, sport utility vehicles (SUVs), 'environmentally friendly' cars, and many others.

Now if you wish to buy a prestigious saloon, for example, perceived quality is likely to be of great importance to you, and you're likely to have an interest in only a few marques. You may well find that the prestige car manufacturers are less willing to offer sizeable price discounts, compared with volume manufacturers. We need to ask where the prestige image comes from. It's partly to do with the sheer quality of the car, but of course it's more than that. The prestige car manufacturer's promotional efforts will make their cars more desirable to you; it's all about branding. And this will obviously make you less price-sensitive. But even then it might be worth persisting, as the case study below indicates.

CASE STUDY: A YORKSHIREMAN SEEKS A DISCOUNT ON A NEW CAR

I have a friend who lives in Yorkshire, and earns a living as a procurement consultant. Now Yorkshire folk are proud of their reputation of being 'like Scotsmen, but without the generous streak', and a disproportionately high number of the leading procurement professionals in the UK hail from the county.

My friend was buying a new car, and he and his wife had decided on the new Mercedes B class. However, his attempts to negotiate with the local main dealer led nowhere. They refused to offer any kind of a price reduction, as the model had just been launched and the dealer was comfortable that sales would be high – so no discount. He decided that a cheaper Japanese vehicle would suffice, and set about looking at different makes and models.

He then had the good idea of speaking to the car fleet manager of one of his clients, who managed a fleet of 300 cars for the company's employees. This person was able to get a written quote from a fleet supplier of Mercedes cars, at a price significantly lower than the price from the local dealership. He walked back into the original dealership armed with the quote and said, 'if you will sell me the same car, and match the price, I will buy it from you'. The salesman then attempted to negotiate upwards, but faced an impossible task. After about 10 minutes, the sales manager agreed to match the price quoted – saving my friend a couple of thousand pounds, for little effort.

The moral of the story is that you don't have to be a fleet buyer to get a great deal – you just have to think like a fleet buyer. It's all about attitude, and arming yourself with market intelligence.

QUALITY

In common parlance, the term 'quality' is used to indicate a scale on which goods and services lie. All else being equal, people would rather have 'high quality' goods and services than 'low quality' goods and services. But of course all else isn't equal, because affordability plays a part – otherwise we'd all be driving around in Mercedes S-class saloons, and travelling on our own private jets for holidays on our islands in the Caribbean, or whatever dream takes your fancy. So a Mercedes S-class saloon is a higher quality car than a Ford, in common parlance. Simple as that.

However, in commercial circles, the term 'quality' is generally taken to mean something quite different, namely consistency with specification. Under this definition, a Mercedes is not necessarily a higher-quality car than a Ford – assuming both have been manufactured to specification.

But we need to go further. One of the key questions we face when defining a buying specification is: 'what does the bought good or service need to achieve?' This is important, because care in answering this question could be important in defining an appropriate buying specification. The topic of buying specifications will be covered in Chapter 3.

TOTAL COST OF OWNERSHIP (TCO)

The TCO concept was developed in recognition of the fact that for some goods, the purchase price may be only the first of a number of costs associated with them; indeed the initial purchase price may be but a small part of the total costs. Hence the term total cost of ownership (TCO). The most important associated costs are the following.

1. Consumables costs

Anyone with a printer at their home or office – particularly a colour printer – will be familiar with this issue. People tend to be shocked when they visit their retailer, and find that the cost of a new set of cartridges may exceed the original cost of the printer. Clearly some way of knowing ink costs before buying the printer would be useful, and the more enlightened manufacturers are starting to recognize that their potential customers have a legitimate interest in the matter.

Now in the case of office copiers rather than printers, the cost of consumables is often not known, because the cost is wrapped up with the costs of repair and maintenance into an overall 'cost per copy'. However, the cumulative copy costs will generally considerably exceed the initial purchase price, particularly for copying equipment processing large volumes.

It follows that in the market-testing process, you need to quote copy volumes for individual machines, and allow the vendors to quote copy costs for individual machines – you will probably find them prepared to offer a lower copy cost on the higher-throughput machines.

2. Maintenance costs

In the case of office copiers and printers, maintenance costs may also be wrapped in with other costs to form a single 'copy cost'. But for a lot of capital equipment, a warranty period will provide for 'free' maintenance and repairs for a period, after which the buyer will pay a stated sum for a maintenance contract, normally a flat sum per year or month.

In the market testing process, you need to seek maintenance costs over the anticipated working life of the equipment. With this data, you'll then be in a position to compare the various vendors' quotations over the anticipated life of the equipment, not just for the initial contract duration or warranty period.

You may find that one or more vendors are unwilling, during the tendering process, to offer post-warranty maintenance contracts. This poses a risk to the buyer, because after the warranty period they may have no choice but to take out a maintenance contract with the vendor (particularly if the vendor has access to spare parts, which may not be readily available from other vendors). The vendor can then 'name their own price', especially if they're aware that the buyer doesn't have a sufficient budget for new equipment. It follows from this that the buyer should have a preference for the vendor who is willing and able to give the lowest costs over the anticipated life of the equipment. After all, isn't that the ultimate vendor statement of confidence in his equipment's performance?

3. Labour costs

There are items of equipment where the associated labour costs are significant in relation to the purchase price, indeed they may dwarf it. A good example is mechanical handling equipment (MHE), such as warehouse forklift trucks. A major global manufacturer of forklift trucks, and a supplier into the UK market, estimates that the TCO of a typical modern electric warehouse forklift truck in the UK can be divided up as follows:

Labour	80%
Equipment costs	10%
Maintenance costs	5%
Energy costs	5%

Now some large warehouses use hundreds of such trucks, of various specifications. You'd have thought that the warehouse managers would work with leading vendors and seek to minimize the TCO, through using reliable, up-to-date equipment – so truck numbers could be minimized, and associated driver numbers likewise. And sometimes this does happen – but all too often the site management simply seeks to drive down the cost of equipment, or keep equipment working well beyond its economic-working life.

4. Energy costs

The use of most capital equipment requires input energy, so energy consumption should be considered when selecting equipment. Commercial vehicles are a good example, and major fleet operators spend considerable time measuring the energy efficiency of their vehicles and maximizing it though careful vehicle selection, driver training etc. Another example is the refrigeration equipment used by retailers. The more enlightened retailers, such as Sainsbury's in the UK, do not buy refrigeration equipment on price and aesthetics alone; they are keen to ensure that energy consumption considerations play an appropriate part in the equipment selection process.

5. Depreciation

For the sake of this section, it's important to recognize that equipment x, with a higher purchase price than equipment y, may have a lower total cost of ownership, for factors beyond those outlined above. This is mainly, but not only, due to the different residual values of different manufacturers' equipment. I refer you a section in Chapter 4, 'Rent rather than buy', for an explanation of this counter-intuitive phenomenon.

3

Effective tools and techniques

Man is a tool-using animal... without tools he is nothing, with tools he is all.

(*Thomas Carlyle:* Sartor Resartus, *1834*)

This chapter contains:

- Spend mapping.
- Estimating and targeting cost reduction opportunities.
- The buying cycle.
- Price benchmarking.
- Specifications – goods.
- Specifications – capital equipment.
- Specifications – services.

A fairly limited number of tools and techniques underpin successful cost reduction efforts. This chapter, along with Chapters 4–6, will outline the most important ones.

Some years ago, one of the largest consultancies in the world had the following mission statement for its procurement consultancy:

- Find the money.
- Get the money.
- Keep the money.

For my money – no pun intended – that had to be one of the best mission statements around. The money they were referring to was the money hidden in the clients' Purchase Ledgers, ie clients' money spent with vendors.

SPEND MAPPING

When a buyer starts work at a new company and their prime objective is cost reduction, they will wish to quickly gain some insights into the company's spend patterns. The process by which they do this is commonly termed 'spend mapping'. The objective of spend mapping is to help the buyer prioritize his cost reduction efforts.

An early 'port of call' will always be the Finance function, to seek data from the Purchase Ledger system. Now the function will not usually analyse data from a supply category perspective, because they are fully occupied with work relating to budgets and cost centres. So the buyer will need to cultivate a good working relationship with staff in the Finance function. The key analyses they will require are the following, and with modern accountancy software packages they are usually readily available. I have often had them within half an hour of requesting them, at new clients: spend by spend category, in descending spend order; and spend by vendor, in descending spend order.

By way of illustration, the following details are drawn from an assignment I carried out for a major professional services firm, with a number of offices around the UK. For the purpose of illustration, I've restricted the first analysis (Table 3.1) to just three of the spend categories which I market tested, namely stationery and print, archiving services and photocopying. The London office's facility manager had negotiated a firm-wide contract for stationery and print, while contracts for the other two areas were negotiated by facilities managers at the individual regional offices.

Table 3.1   Spend by spend category, in descending spend order

Spend category	Annual spend	Responsible manager
Stationery and print	£1.28 million	TS (London)
Archiving services	£590,000	Individual office managers
Photocopying	£450,000	Individual office managers

Table 3.2 shows the second analysis:

Table 3.2   Spend by vendor, in descending spend order

Vendor	Annual spend	Responsible manager
Stationery and print		
Johnson Stationery Ltd	£1.28 million	TS (London)
Archiving services		
Store Here Ltd	£230,000	TS (London)
Economic Storage Ltd	£150,000	JA (Manchester)
Document Storage Ltd	£120,000	GB (Cardiff); TS (London); JM (Glasgow)
Costsaver Ltd	£90,000	JM (Glasgow)
Photocopying		
Xerox Ltd	£110,000	TS (London); GB (Cardiff); JM (Glasgow)
Ricoh Ltd	£80,000	JA (Manchester)
Surecopy Ltd	£75,000	JM (Glasgow)
Mortimer Office Equipment Ltd	£60,000	TS (London); JA (Manchester)
Perfect Copy Ltd	£50,000	GB (Cardiff)
Canon Ltd	£45,000	TS (London); JM (Glasgow)
Toshiba Ltd	£20,000	JA (Manchester)
Sharp Ltd	£10,000	GB (Cardiff)

Analyses of this type raise a number of questions for a buyer seeking to reduce costs, including:

- What are the buying competences of the individual facility managers?
- What is the rationale, if any, for the number of vendors in each category (stationery and print = 1, archiving services = 4, photocopying = 8)?
- Is there a sound rationale for the division of business between the vendors? Or has this simply come about over time, on an ad hoc basis?
- What has been the performance of the different vendors? Which poorly performing vendors should be dropped from consideration for future business?
- What might be done to concentrate the business with fewer vendors, to reduce costs? Might sole sourcing be viable for archiving and copiers?

- What decision-making processes have led to vendor selection?
- What market-testing exercises have taken place in these areas, if any? What were the conclusions of these exercises?
- What contracts are in place, and what contract terms might limit the forward contracting options over time?
- Are there major viable vendors in the marketplaces, which might bring economies of scale into play, and deliver goods and services at markedly lower prices?

The detailed case studies are provided at the end of Chapter 5, and the reader is urged to read them now. Through asking questions such as the above, and carrying out market-testing exercises, significant savings were delivered – as outlined in Table 3.3.

Table 3.3 Savings delivered to a UK professional services firm

Spend area	Annual spend	Savings as a proportion of spend	Annual savings
Stationery and printed materials	£1,280,000	39.1%	£500,000
Archiving services	£590,000	20.3%	£120,000
Photocopying	£450,000	22.2%	£100,000
TOTALS	£2,320,000	31.0%	£720,000

ESTIMATING AND TARGETING COST SAVINGS OPPORTUNITIES

Buyers looking for cost reductions are likely to be faced with a large number of spend areas they could address. But with limited resources, they are forced to prioritize their efforts. How might they best do this?

I often find myself facing this very question at the outset of an assignment, and my approach is based on combining three assessments:

- the intrinsic cost reduction potential within individual spend areas (this subject was covered in Chapter 2);
- the client's recent buying effort and expertise applied to the area;
- supply market difficulty, most notably the number of viable vendors with adequate capacity to serve my client's needs.

Now I use the three assessments to help me estimate the cost reduction potential in each spend area. First, I decide whether the intrinsic cost-savings potential is low, moderate or high, and then forecast potential percentage cost savings for each spend area, from the matrices shown in Figures 3.1, 3.2 and 3.3.

To illustrate how the methodology works in practice, I'll again draw upon data from the professional services client I've just mentioned. After discussions with the key executives and meetings with some of the incumbent and non-incumbent vendors, I felt in a position to forecast the savings potential in each of the three areas. Table 3.4 shows how the forecasted potential compared with the actual cost savings delivered. It will be noted that there is a fair gap between forecast and actual savings – actual savings being higher in two of the three cases. Such variability is commonly found in cost reduction programmes. My strong advice is not to allow the estimated cost reduction potential, in a given spend area, to act as a ceiling on your ambitions.

The application of this methodology to all the significant spend areas will lead to a league table of cost reduction opportunities, and therefore provide a guide to buyer effort prioritization.

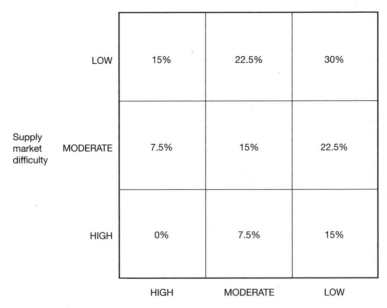

Figure 3.1   *Matrix of cost reduction potential when intrinsic cost reduction potential is HIGH*

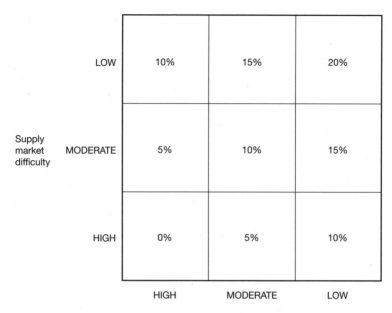

	HIGH	MODERATE	LOW
LOW	10%	15%	20%
MODERATE	5%	10%	15%
HIGH	0%	5%	10%

Supply market difficulty

Recent effort and expertise focused on this spend area

Figure 3.2   _Matrix of cost reduction potential when intrinsic cost reduction potential is MODERATE_

	HIGH	MODERATE	LOW
LOW	5%	7.5%	10%
MODERATE	2.5%	5%	7.5%
HIGH	0%	2.5%	5%

Supply market difficulty

Recent effort and expertise focused on this spend area

Figure 3.3   _Matrix of cost reduction potential when intrinsic cost reduction potential is LOW_

Table 3.4 Comparison between forecast cost reduction potential and actual savings delivery at a UK professional services firm

Spend area	Annual spend	Intrinsic cost reduction potential	Supply market difficulty	Effort and expertise applied by client	Cost-savings potential forecast	Annual cost-savings potential forecast	Cost savings actually delivered	Annual cost savings actually delivered
Stationery and print	£1,280,000	High	Low	Low	30%	£384,000	39.1%	£500,000
Archiving services	£590,000	Moderate	Moderate	Low	15%	£88,500	20.3%	£120,000
Photocopying	£450,000	High	Low	Low	30%	£135,000	22.2%	£100,000
TOTALS	£2,320,000				26.2%	£607,500	31.0%	£720,000

One tricky question arises if you are intending to apply this method-ology yourself, without the support of a procurement expert, namely: what 'effort and expertise' has been applied in recent times? If you have carried out some work yourself, you will be inclined to rate effort and expertise as 'moderate' or 'high'. My advice is to rate it 'low', however, to raise your ambition level. Procurement experts will almost always come up with a 'low' assessment for individuals who are not long steeped in the discipline. Sorry!

THE BUYING CYCLE

This is the term commonly used by buyers to describe the sequence of distinct stages involved in the buying process. It enables them to maintain control of the process and allocate their time appropriately, thereby helping to avoid the time pressures that might otherwise lead to poor buying decisions.

The buying cycle starts by defining the corporate objectives (such as cost reduction) that may be supported or enabled by a company's rela-tionships with its vendors, and the steps it takes to secure the optimal contractual relationships and business relationships. It ends with management of the contract which results from the process. But the next buying cycle must start before the current contract end date.

The sheer effort involved in adoption of the buying cycle may surprise you, as will the fact that there are as many as 12 stages involved. But the full cycle should only be used for significant projects, which may be defined as those projects with objectives that merit the effort, for example:

- major cost reductions;
- competitive advantage;
- risk reduction (legal, operational, commercial).

Organizations that are seeking to improve their buying performance invariably find it a challenging task, and tend to consider relatively few options, usually those that appear by popular consensus to have served them well in the past. I find that approaches resulting from this 'line of least resistance' are usually sub-optimal, and a more rigorous approach – the adoption of the buying cycle process for major projects – will deliver stronger results.

The buying cycle process is as valid for the buying of services as it is for the buying of goods. The nature of individual spend areas will clearly have a bearing on the detailed approach to be taken, as well as the effort, experience and expertise applied to the area in the recent past. However, for most major projects, most of the stages will be required. Smaller projects and one-off purchases may well merit less effort. The buying cycle stages are as follows.

1. Define the objectives

The broad objectives of the company's efforts in individual areas may be suggested by the buying portfolio (covered in Chapter 2). Objectives definition is a challenging task, and will generally require dialogue with senior colleagues.

2. Define organizational requirements

Operational and/or technical specialists frequently have a key role in defining organizational needs, specifications, service level agreements and key performance indicators. In some companies, a lack of information (eg on demand, expenditure, existing contractual commitments) may well be a problem. If this is the case, one of the key objectives of initial contracts will be the delivery of detailed management information, which will enhance the quality of the next buying cycle.

3. Define information needs, and develop a project plan

This stage will involve internal data analysis, and confirming the commitment of senior managers. In organizations where some end-users might not comply with the final contract – for whatever reasons – it needs to be agreed at this stage that the final contracts will be mandatory for end-users.

In larger organizations, especially those with a number of operational locations, it is vital to stop local deals being made once there is a whiff of HQ interest in the spend area. A clear instruction from the CEO will usually save a good deal of wasted time and frustration.

Some sense of the time the project may require will now be emerging, so it is a good point at which to develop a draft project plan. All too often, managers find they have inadequate time in which to develop and execute the project. The result is that numerous key stages are skipped or carried out poorly, resulting in a sub-optimal contract at the end. Be generous when setting time for the overall buying cycle. Unforeseen problems and opportunities may arise during the cycle, and time will be required to explore them.

4. Undertake market research

The scale of the research effort will be determined by the nature of the marketplace, the resources available, and the benefits expected to flow from the project. Key issues to be considered include potential vendor financial viability, capacity and capability. A note of warning: some executives believe the internet has taken the effort out of developing a list of potential vendors, but this is rarely the case. Chapter 5 will cover the subject of market testing, including buying from overseas vendors, and Chapter 9 will cover the subject of e-procurement.

This is the stage during which you should aim to gain a comprehensive understanding of how the particular market works, through meeting with a number of vendors and encouraging and allowing them to put forward innovative solutions and approaches. It could be that you're happy to work with vendors in the manner they wish, but my firm advice would be to explore options for gaining more benefits and reducing your risks. Only a few vendors may be prepared, in the final analysis, to go along with your preferred way of working, but that may be enough. Don't worry about the majority complaining that you're being unfair. You're paid to be unfair, a point I'll explain in the context of negotiation, in Chapter 7.

5. Formally contact the selected potential vendors

The formal method of communication might be an RFI (request for information), an RFP (request for proposal), an ITT (invitation to tender), or an alternative approach. This subject is covered in Chapter 5, and an RFP template is provided in Appendix 2. It also available online at www.lpsconsulting.co.uk.

6. Develop the draft contract, with appropriate terms and conditions

Professional buyers will need no reminding of the importance of well-constructed contracts, but in many organizations managers seek to avoid formal contracts, usually in the mistaken belief that this improves their flexibility. In reality, in the absence of a formal contract, companies tend to be bound by the vendors' contract terms, often as a result of the vendors' order acknowledgements. The buyer's weak position may only become clear when they try to cease ordering from a particular vendor. Contractual issues are covered in Chapter 8.

7. Vendor response stage

Vendors frequently report that companies take a great deal of time in developing a tender, then expect a response in a very short timeframe. This is unfortunate, given the relationship between response quality and the time available. Given that the overall buying cycle tends to be a lengthy process, a reasonable time should be allowed for this stage.

8. Analyse vendor responses, develop a shortlist, resolve any areas of uncertainty

Again, a reasonable time should be allowed for this stage, particularly for complex spend areas. Vendors are generally more willing to really apply themselves to a potential contract once they know they are on the shortlist.

9. Undertake contractual and commercial negotiations, construct the final contract with fully developed Terms and Conditions

Negotiation is the subject of Chapter 7, contracts and contract law the subjects of Chapter 8. The quality of negotiation planning and execution in many organizations is lamentable. Salespeople invariably receive far more negotiation training than the buyers they face, and the content of many contracts is a stark testament to this reality.

10. Award contracts, communicate details around the organization

Once the contract has been signed by both parties, it is time for the buyer to communicate the salient details around their organization, possibly through an intranet. The mandatory nature of the contract needs to be made explicit to end-users.

11. Complete a buying cycle review document

This document will be a record of the processes undertaken, the thinking behind the final approach, market analysis, data analysis etc. The document will be of considerable assistance when the category is to be addressed again, particularly if a new person becomes responsible for the spend area.

12. Manage the contract

Contract management is a critical activity, ensuring that both parties fulfil their obligations under the contract. The key objectives for the buyer include:

- ensuring the vendor delivers the right good(s) and/or service(s) to the agreed place(s) at the agreed time(s), at the agreed price(s);
- ensuring the vendor delivers the required management information in a timely fashion;
- maintaining good relations and communications between end-users and the vendor;
- identifying and managing risks.

For many spend areas, operational and/or technical specialists may have a key role in contract management, possibly through some form of post-contract review process. In addition, a mechanism might usefully be introduced to enable end-users to comment on their experience of the contract.

At an appropriate time before contract expiry, the buying cycle should start again. If left too late, the buyer will be exposed to time pressures where, for example, alternative vendors cannot start supplying until after the current contract expires. This could give the current vendor considerable power, and force the buyer to negotiate a contract extension from a weak position. A simple process for ensuring that such scenarios do not arise, the contract register, is described in Chapter 8.

In conclusion, executing the buying cycle process will be a challenge, particularly for individuals and companies unused to a formal multi-stage approach to buying. The keys to success are careful planning and execution, and the outcome will invariably justify the effort involved.

PRICE BENCHMARKING

This term refers to the practice of comparing existing price levels with the price levels apparently being paid by other buyers. Some buyers are keen on this methodology, often because it highlights where they are paying a good deal more for a good or service than other buyers. And for this very reason, the methodology may be of some value to 'rookie buyers'. But I am sceptical about the potential value of price benchmarking, for a number of reasons.

Sources of data

Where does the data come from? If from a competitor, why would they simply hand over pricing data that has presumably resulted from some effort on their part, to obtain the best pricing possible for their company? This would arguably be a dereliction of duty on their part, and probably also in contravention of both the letter and spirit of the confidentiality clause found in most commercial contracts.

Fewer objections can be made if the source of the data is not a competitor.

Comparability of data

Even if pricing data is accurate, what does this tell you? After all, just because a vendor sells a particular good or service to another company at a given price, it hardly follows that he would be prepared to supply you at the same price. Many factors go into vendors' price-setting strategies. And who is to say your competitor's buyer is buying competently? Don't forget, the performance of 50 per cent of buyers is below average.

Impact on resources

Time is always in short supply. I would almost always prefer to spend my time investigating supply markets, and meeting current and potential new vendors, rather than undertaking a price-benchmarking exercise. That way, I'm raising my knowledge of the market and its vendors, which is one of the keys to obtaining lower prices.

Impact on ambition

On occasion I've come across buyers who have found an apparently genuine price benchmark for a good or service. In most cases, an interesting thing happens. The buyer has no ambition to seek a price lower than the benchmark. It doesn't even occur to them that the vendor might be quite prepared to supply them at a lower price, if the buyer were to execute a sound market-testing exercise.

Vendors' influence on pricing data

Some years ago I walked into the offices of a new client, the day after the head of procurement had been fired. It took me very little time to realize quite how incompetent he had been – far worse than the client had judged – and I was able to make swift progress in a number of areas.

But one area puzzled me. The company converted numerous polymers (eg polypropylene) into a range of goods, and the company received a weekly update on polymer pricing, via an independent 'market report'. The company was a very small buyer of some polymers, and yet apparently the incompetent head of purchasing had been buying them at a price in line with large buyers in the marketplace. What could explain this? An investigation led to the following conclusions: market pricing was lower than that given in the market report, due to a combination of calculated mis-reporting by major sellers and major buyers; and most buyers were contractually committed to buying the raw materials from the vendors at or near the price reported in the independent market reports – so the buyers' pricing was following the report, rather than vice versa!

SPECIFICATIONS – GOODS

Sound specification setting is at the heart of professional buying. Without a clear specification, how can you know exactly what it is that you're buying, or complain after delivery that 'it' – whether it be a good or a service – is not acceptable? The responsibility for ensuring adequacy of specification rests with the buyer.

But there's one obvious problem. Buyers cannot be expected to be 'technical experts' on the multitude of goods and services they buy, although they may have colleagues who can fulfil the role in some spend areas. So buyers are usually at the mercy of vendors, who may seem to 'hold all the cards' in this area.

With a little effort, however, much progress can be made to counter the problem. To illustrate the point, let's take a simple example, copier paper. In Chapter 1, we came across a basic specification for office copier paper, reproduced below in Table 3.5.

Table 3.5   Basic specification for copier paper

Characteristics	Test method	Values	Tolerances
Substance	ISO 536	80 gsm	± 0.5 gsm
Thickness	ISO 534	104 microns	± 3 microns
Surface roughness	ISO 8791–2	233 ml/min	± 2 ml/min
Whiteness	ISO 11475	142	± 4
Opacity	ISO 2471	90%	± 2%

Now there are a number of other specification elements (or 'character-istics') we could add, but these will suffice for our purpose. It's worth spending some time to understand what the table is actually telling us.

Characteristics

The first three characteristics are important for the smooth running of the paper through modern copiers, while the final two relate to aesthetic considerations. All five characteristics are arguably important with respect to the perceived quality of the paper – we'll come on to the subject of quality shortly.

The characteristic I find people most people confused about, with respect to paper specifications, is substance. They often believe the value of 80 gsm relates to the paper's thickness, while it is in fact a measure of paper density when related to the stated thickness, quite obvious given the meaning of the term 'gsm', ie grammes per square metre. So for a given paper thickness (say 104 microns), a paper with a 10 per cent higher substance will be 10 per cent more dense.

Test methods

ISO is an acronym for the International Standards Organization, and a 'test method' is simply the process by which a characteristic is measured, so two laboratories in different places, at different times, should obtain the same results for the same material.

Values

The value of the characteristic as measured by the specified test method. Of itself, of limited value – it needs to be considered in association with the tolerance.

Tolerances

Many specifications fail to include tolerances, and this is a serious omission. To illustrate, a specification for copier paper may state a value of 80 gsm, but an independent test may show a sample of delivered paper to be only 70 gsm. The manufacturer or wholesaler is likely to retort that this is within 'manufacturing tolerances'. This is, in fact, complete nonsense. Copier paper is manufactured to an extremely tight tolerance, as one would expect in such a competitive marketplace.

The quoted specification was obtained from a major office products retailer, and you'll see the tolerance is 0.5 gsm. So the retailer is stating that the paper's substance will lie between 79.5 gsm and 80.5 gsm.

The key point is that if there are no stated tolerances, or the stated tolerances are sizeable, it gives a 'green light' to vendors that they can supply goods which are inferior to those the buyer may be expecting.

SPECIFICATIONS – CAPITAL EQUIPMENT

Many of the issues surrounding capital goods buying are found with the buying of office copiers, and copiers will be familiar to every reader, so I'll use them to illustrate a number of points. A buyer charged with buying copiers may be bewildered by the differences between equipment from the potential vendors, including:

- equipment costs;
- costs per copy;
- copying speed;
- paper tray numbers and capacities;
- paper size options;
- maximum number of originals;
- compatible material gauges;
- mono/colour copying;
- facility for limiting costly colour prints, to minimize abuse;
- networking capabilities, eg could the equipment double as a printer for office staff working nearby?
- stacking options;
- stapling options, eg position, maximum number of sheets;
- faxing capability;
- equipment 'footprint' – floor area required;
- energy consumption, while operating and while on 'standby';
- warm-up time from 'standby'.

The buyer must also consider a number of other issues:

- Appropriateness of equipment specifications to requirements – eg an office location with copy volumes of 50,000 copies per month will normally require a faster copier than a location with 5,000 copies per month.
- What is the relative 'user friendliness' of the different vendors' equipment?

- All else being equal, end-users prefer to remain with the current manufacturer's equipment range, to minimize their 'learning curve'.
- Equipment reliability – what percentage of office working hours must the machine be available for, with full functionality? What engineer response time is required in the event of a problem?
- What if spare parts become unavailable during the contract term?

It is clearly beyond the scope of this book to address all these issues, but I will address two areas where I find clients have experienced the most trouble in their previous dealings with copier vendors.

1. Comparing different vendors' offerings

This is the classic 'apples and pears' issue. Vendor x's equipment is 10 per cent more expensive than vendor y's, but vendor x's salesman maintains this is because their equipment is more advanced technically, and proceeds to 'blind the buyer with science', in line with their training.

Time and again, in a given client situation, I've found that one vendor stands out from the crowd, in having a highly ethical and professional approach to the client in question. The vendor may or may not be the current vendor. My usual practice is to have that vendor carry out a number of tasks:

- survey historical copy volumes, by machine, so as to determine appropriate equipment models, and locations;
- meet with key users and myself, to develop some idea of technical requirements;
- propose machine models, and provide detailed technical specifications on each model.

The technical specifications from such an exercise will be somewhat more detailed than you might expect, and Table 3.6 illustrates an example developed by a vendor for a 45 ppm (45 pages per minute) machine.

With such a detailed specification, you are now in a position to develop the tender document, in which you will stipulate that the vendor's equipment must meet all the minimum specification elements, and where it does not, the vendor is required to point out the discrepancy in their tender response. Through this approach, you will go a long way to resolving the 'apples and pears' problem.

In the case of sizeable orders for smaller capital goods such as copiers, you may well find that the vendors are willing to provide machines for comparative tests at your location. I carried out a comparison of five

Table 3.6 Minimum specification requirements for a 45 ppm copier

Type		Standalone copier
Maximum original size		A3
Copy sizes	cassette	A5R–A3
	stack bypass	A3–A6
Resolution	copying	1200 dpi equivalent × 600 dpi
Copy speed	A4	45 ppm
	A3	22 ppm
	first copy time	less than 3.9 seconds
	warm-up time	30 sec max (10 sec max from sleep mode)
	multiple copies/prints	1 to 999 sheets
	duplexing	standard automatic stackless
Paper weight	cassette	64 to 80 gsm
	stack bypass	64 to 128 gsm
Dimensions	W × D × H	565 × 700 × 761 mm
Cassette	universal	A5R to A3
Paper capacity	standard	550 sheets × 2 cassettes (1,100 sheets) multi stack bypass : 50 sheets (80 gsm)
	optional extra	550 sheets × 2 cassettes (1,100 sheets)
	CPU	300 MHz
	memory	256 MB (Max 512 MB)
	hard disk drive	20 GB
	power supply	230 V/6A/50 Hz
	power consumption (W)	1.0 kW maximum
	energy consumption	39 W/h
Document feeder	paper size	A3–A5R
	single sided original	42 to 128 gsm
	double sided original	50 to 128 gsm
	max number of originals	50 sheets (80 gsm)
	copy	28 ppm
Finishing	number of trays	one stack tray
	tray capacity	A4–A5R: 1,000 sheets A3: 500 sheets
	staple position	corner
	staple capacity	A4: 50 sheets A3: 30 Sheets

vendors' equipment for a major professional services firm in 2006, and was struck by the differences in performance (eg the times to complete various defined tasks). Many of these differences could not have been picked up through even the lengthiest review of the vendors' specification sheets.

2. Equipment reliability and engineer response time

Apart from technical specification issues, salespeople will often try to justify a price premium for their equipment, saying it is attributable to one or both of the following areas: superior build quality, hence better reliability; faster engineer response times.

Now these assertions may or not be true, but it would be a naive buyer who took the assertions on trust. Fast engineer response times are not in themselves much use if the engineer does not fix the problem on a high proportion of first visits.

The challenge for the buyer is to enshrine high equipment uptime (say, a minimum of 98 per cent of office working hours) into the contract terms. And a failure on the part of the vendor to ensure high equipment uptime will result in financial compensation being made to the buyer, or – in the case of individual problematical machines – substitute machines being supplied to the buyer at no additional cost to the buyer. The 'financial compensation' will need to result from a liquidated damages clause in the UK.

In this age of reliable digital copiers, the time take for preventative maintenance should be regarded as downtime.

SPECIFICATIONS – SERVICES

Companies frequently find buying services more difficult than buying goods, for a range of reasons:

- They struggle to define services to the extent necessary for market testing.
- Performance is often difficult to measure, and data difficult to obtain.
- Where the service is complex (eg legal advice), the buyer may struggle to differentiate between potential vendors.
- The buyer may feel it important to have a close relationship with, say, their legal advice supplier, which they would probably not require with their office stationery supplier.

Where it is fairly challenging to describe a service specification for the purpose of ensuring service delivery, it is customary to develop a service level agreement (SLA), which describes the service required. Within the SLA there will usually be key performance indicators (KPIs), which may or may not be numerical in nature. It is important to realize that the SLA is not the contract between the two parties, but it is associated with the contract, and the contract will refer to it in some key areas. Most importantly, the contract will outline the buyer's right to terminate the contract, should the vendor's performance fall below that required by the SLA.

The outline of a service level agreement I negotiated for a client, with a major UK printer, is provided in Appendix 1, and it also available online at www.lpsconsulting.co.uk. Now while printed materials are clearly 'goods', there was a very clear need to document the service requirements in the complex contract. This particular SLA covers numerous issues, including:

- introduction – background, purpose, scope, terms of reference, authorized representatives, process;
- service levels – one-off print items, print stock items;
- packaging, labelling, delivery and service measures;
- customer service and support;
- invoicing;
- management information;
- competitiveness;
- conformance;
- value-added and proactive management;
- management of change in style/format/branding;
- management reviews;
- key performance indicators – for measuring the vendor's operational performance;
- key performance indicators – for improving operational performance.

The level of detail required within individual SLAs will clearly depend on a number of factors.

4

The changes that deliver cost reduction

*When faced with the choice between changing and proving there's
no need to do so, most people get busy on the proof.*

(John K Galbraith)

This chapter contains:

- Engage the current vendor(s), and potential new vendors.
- Change WHAT is bought.
- Change HOW it is bought.
- Change WHEN it is bought.
- Change WHO buys it.
- Change WHERE you buy it from.
- Rent rather than buy?
- Involve procurement at an earlier stage in the buying cycle.

If a company is going to achieve cost reductions beyond those it already
has planned, it needs to make some changes. But what changes? The
options are not infinite, but this chapter covers the majority of them.

ENGAGE THE CURRENT VENDOR(S), AND POTENTIAL NEW VENDORS

I find this an invaluable way to understand how costs may be reduced. You need to meet not only the current vendor(s), but also potential vendors. The latter, after all, have everything to gain, and nothing to lose.

The principle is quite simple. You inform the current vendor(s) that in line with cost reduction targets you've been set, you're looking to satisfy your requirements for the goods or services in question, at a price markedly less than you're currently paying, say 20 per cent less. And stress that you're not looking to 'meet halfway', you want the full reduction. The extent of the cost reduction you're seeking will largely be dictated by the intrinsic cost reduction potential of the spend area in question (Chapter 2), and the market difficulty and recent effort and expertise applied to the area (Chapter 3). If in doubt, aim for a somewhat higher cost reduction than you believe could possibly be achievable. And tell the current vendor that you're speaking to other vendors, to get a better sense of what options are available. This should galvanize them into taking the matter seriously.

The current vendor is in the fortunate position of knowing your buying patterns in detail, and they obviously know their own economics in supplying the good or service. So they are in a good position to advise what can be changed in order to reduce their costs, some or all of which can be passed on to you. Or maybe they will just have to reduce the profit they realize on their business with your organization. Examples of using vendor input are provided in a number of the case studies in this chapter.

As far as potential new vendors are concerned, you need to give them an outline of the goods or services involved, then ask them for options to reduce costs. You may be able to use some of their ideas within the market-testing process, which will generally follow this stage.

CHANGE *WHAT* IS BOUGHT

Specification/service level agreement (SLA) modification

One of the great pleasures in being a consultant is being able to ask the simple – even 'stupid' – questions, which clients' executives wouldn't think of asking. The following case study provides an example.

CASE STUDY: THE PHONE CALL THAT SAVED £60,000 PA

Looking at a new client's office stationery sometimes gives me a good 'feel' for how the company buys. On my first day working at a professional services firm in 2006, I noticed the firm was buying its letterhead with a bespoke watermark, ie one that was unique to them – the watermark was the logo adopted on the merger of two firms into one, the previous year.

I knew that bespoke watermarks were expensive, and therefore not common in commercial organizations, and soon learnt that the firm was paying a 67 per cent premium for it, over the same paper without a watermark – £150,000 pa as opposed to £90,000 pa, ie a premium of £60,000 pa. I asked the buyer concerned if it could possibly be removed on future orders, and he was adamant it couldn't be – 'The head of business development would have a fit!'

I called the head of business development. It turned out he hadn't been made aware that a premium was payable for the watermark, and upon being told of the cost premium, he agreed that it be dropped forthwith. A £60,000 pa saving had resulted from asking one simple question.

In some spend areas, a great deal of money may be saved by moving from branded to generic, 'own label' goods. An obvious example is office stationery. The leading office stationery companies have high-quality own label products which match or nearly match the performance of branded goods, usually at considerably lower prices.

There are few goods and services whose cost cannot be reduced through a change in specification. Vendors will be in the best position to take you through the options available.

Reduce consumption

The possibility of reducing consumption varies with spend area, but there are sometimes good opportunities. This is a time to be creative, and ask questions such as 'how might we use x per cent less of this good/service?', and 'what would happen if we used x per cent less of this good/service?' Two examples should illustrate the point: 1) develop an energy efficiency campaign – quite apart from the environmental benefits, the financial returns might well be higher than you'd expect; 2) communicate with customers and potential customers more through websites and e-mail, and thereby reduce your purchases of printed materials.

CHANGE _HOW_ IT IS BOUGHT

Change ordering patterns – take advantage of vendors' internal economics

It could be that your ordering patterns result in high costs for your vendor, which they have to pass on to you. And it follows that if you change your ordering patterns, the vendor could reduce their prices. For example, for manufactured goods, it may be possible to aggregate future requirements into fewer, longer production runs. This is especially likely to be a profitable approach where the items in question are custom-manufactured to your requirements, and manufacturing equipment set-up costs are high.

Now it could be, for example, that you buy a range of packaging, where the only difference across the range is the print element. The manufacturer might be able to save manufacturing time (and therefore money) if they were to produce several designs sequentially – or even simultaneously, depending on the print method concerned. The following case study illustrates the point.

CASE STUDY: CHANGING ORDERING PATTERNS FOR LABELS SAVES £150,000 PA

Company: FMCG manufacturer
Spend area: Self-adhesive labels
Annual spend: £600,000
Summary: The introduction of fewer, longer production runs, along with an appropriate pricing technique, led to cost savings in excess of £150,000 pa (25 per cent).

Background

I asked the vendor to put forward options to reduce label prices by 25 per cent. They duly proposed a number of material and print specification changes, but none were acceptable to my company's marketing department. But the vendor pointed out another way to reduce prices.

My company bought a wide variety of labels for the toiletry products it manufactured. For a given product range and size, the labels would be of a consistent size and shape, only the print would vary. Given the fast-moving nature of the FMCG marketplace, demand at the individual label level was highly erratic, leading to damaging stock shortages, which were traditionally resolved either by costly short label production runs, or by holding high stock levels (which in turn led to costly obsolescence). A great deal of administration was involved for both parties, in ordering and pricing.

A meeting with the vendor identified that printing equipment set-up times were lengthy, and accordingly expensive. The set-up costs could represent 90 per cent+ of overall costs, for short production runs. If the overall order lengths (of a given label size and shape) could be increased, costs would fall.

Action taken

The SUPAR (Set-up and Run-on) pricing technique was introduced. Each Friday a review of stock levels and forthcoming demand was translated into an order for labels to be manufactured the following Monday, and delivered the following day. The SUPAR formulae led to exact label pricing being known in advance of ordering.

Outcome

The new ordering process dramatically reduced the number of times the vendor was required to set up their machines for short print runs, and stock shortages and obsolescence fell sharply. Over £150,000 (25 per cent) was saved in the first year alone, through the introduction of this technique. In addition, the administrative load on both parties was greatly reduced.

Recognize that budgeting practices can lead to sub-optimal decision making

This opportunity often results from the 'total cost of ownership' issue outlined in Chapter 2. It often happens that one budget-holder's budget is impacted by the activities or decisions of other budget-holders. So when one budget-holder drives their costs down, they may sometimes do so at the expense of other budget-holders.

A good example is the refrigeration cabinets bought by grocery retailers. In some retailers, the buying of refrigeration cabinets is carried out by an individual or department charged with minimizing equipment costs, but with no brief to consider energy consumption. The result is predictable – the savings made by buying cheap cabinets tend to be dwarfed by the extra costs of the additional electricity consumed by them. The more enlightened retailers (such as Sainsbury's supermarkets, Appendix 5) adopt the 'total cost of ownership' approach.

Introduce sound asset management practices

Many companies pay far too little attention to improving asset utilization, particularly where the company has a large number of sites, and possibly a number of different business units. The following case study is about an exercise I carried out some years ago.

CASE STUDY: SURVEYS AND ASSET MANAGEMENT SAVE A LOGISTICS COMPANY £500,000 PA

Company: Logistics company
Spend area: Materials handling equipment (MHE)
Annual spend: £10 million
Summary: Sites wishing to order new MHE – capital equipment such as forklift trucks – were required to have the approved vendor undertake a fleet utilization survey to ensure a real demand existed, and then check whether suitable surplus equipment already existed within the organization, which could be transferred. The two processes led to a reduction of 30 per cent in new asset acquisitions, saving in excess of £500,000 pa.

Background

The organization had over 300 sites in the UK, most with MHE, from 1 to 150 items. When a site required further pieces of equipment, it contacted the approved vendor and ordered equipment at contract prices, under agreed contract terms. It became apparent that sites were on occasion ordering equipment when existing asset utilization was not high, and/or where there was surplus equipment available in other parts of the organization. No mechanism existed to link sites requiring new equipment with sites which had surplus equipment.

Action taken

Discussions with the vendor led to an agreed process defining when site surveys would be conducted, to establish whether the new items were genuinely required, or whether there might be alternative solutions. The vendor also introduced, and maintained, a central database of surplus equipment, and made it available to all sites on the company intranet. Site managers could then readily locate surplus equipment of the type they were seeking.

Outcome

The two initiatives (site surveys and central database introduction) each had a significant impact on the number of new machines acquired. It was estimated that the number of new machines ordered was reduced by around 30 per cent, saving in excess of £500,000 pa.

Renegotiate existing contracts

I commonly find new clients committed to a number of commercially poor contracts. But vendors are often willing to renegotiate such contracts, particularly if the prize is a longer-term contract, albeit at lower price levels.

Ensure compliance with centrally negotiated contracts

Companies often go to the substantial effort and expense of having a central procurement function, negotiating contracts for some spend areas across the organization, and they then experience a lack of compliance at a local level – so-called 'maverick buying' – where local managers continue to use their own preferred vendors. There are two schools of thought on how to deal with this issue: 1) It is the responsibility of the central procurement function to ensure compliance, through improving communications with local operations, and persuading them of the case for the central deal; 2) it is the responsibility of the senior management of the firm to ensure local compliance with central contracts.

The first school of thought has been in the ascendant for some years, but to my mind it begs the question of the validity of a central procurement function in the first place. It also raises the issue of whether spending much time 'selling' is a good use of the function's limited resources. Would a central finance function have to continually 'justify its existence' in this way? Of course not.

I have seen a number of firms take an interesting and pragmatic approach to this thorny issue in recent years. They 'freeze' the list of suppliers at a given point in time, after which local managers need to get the approval of the central procurement department for the addition of any vendors to the list. Given that any non-approved vendors will not get their invoices paid, the problem of maverick buying should decrease quickly.

Capitalize on vendors' willingness to cut prices for time-sensitive services

We're all familiar with the 'lastminute.com' principle, ie vendors will be willing to reduce their prices for services where there is a risk that they would otherwise not be sold at all. The principle is generally applicable in scenarios where the vendor faces low variable costs, and high fixed costs, in providing the service. So, for a hotel room, the variable costs of providing the room are low – the services of a cleaner, laundry services, utilities – but the fixed costs are high.

The buyer needs to consider which of their spend areas might be of a time-sensitive nature. I once saved a considerable sum of money for a logistics company, after recognizing that the principle would apply well to ferry services on routes where there was competition between two or more different operators.

Capitalize on vendors' periods of low demand

In many markets, for both services and goods, vendors have periods of low demand (seasonal, time of week, even time of day), and may accept lower pricing to improve capacity utilization.

One source of cost reduction that companies consider all too rarely is taking advantage of vendors' seasonal demands. That is, there could be merit in learning about vendors' busy and less busy periods, with a view to reducing costs in the less busy periods. The following case study is an example of an exercise I carried out for a major logistics company, which saved them over £500,000 pa.

CASE STUDY: INTRODUCING SEASONAL PRICING FOR TRAILERS SAVES A LOGISTICS COMPANY £500,000 PA

Company: Logistics company
Spend area: Trailer rental
Annual spend: £3.0 million
Summary: In excess of £500,000 pa (16 per cent) overall cost reductions were achieved with the introduction of a detailed operational specification, and seasonal pricing.

Background

The trailer rental market is highly seasonal. For many specifications there are sizeable demand peaks, notably at Christmas, when availability may fall to zero, or close to it. Spot pricing is highly dependent on individual vendors' fleet utilization levels.

The company had an in-house trailer management operation, which supplied a moderate (but declining) proportion of the company's needs. The manager of the operation was also responsible for negotiating terms with third-party providers. He was demanding both stable pricing through the year and high levels of availability in the peak season. In addition, there were considerable differences between the vendors with regard to exactly what was covered by the contracts, in areas such as tyre wear levels and costs, breakdown responsiveness, time to notify damage etc. Such issues frequently led to time-consuming arguments with vendors.

Action taken

Working with key vendors, I developed a detailed operational specification which not only covered key operational issues, but was also judged as likely to be accepted by the majority of available vendors – a key issue.

I developed a tender, with highly detailed contract terms, which sought pricing for three 'seasons' (January–March, April–September, October–December).

Outcome

The vendors welcomed having an operational specification for the first time. While peak season rates remained largely unchanged, rates between January and September fell dramatically in a number of cases. The resulting cost savings were estimated at over £500,000 pa.

Ensure appropriate relationships with vendors

There are a few areas of spend for most companies where the effort to develop partnerships with vendors may be justifiable, eg where outstanding levels of vendor input may lead to competitive advantage. Partnerships with vendors are not appropriate for highly competitive markets with perennial over-supply.

Use e-procurement solutions, eg e-auctions

The savings claimed by service providers are substantial, often 10–50 per cent, and sometimes even more. The higher savings claims tend to reflect the impact of attention to spend areas with high intrinsic cost-savings potential (Chapter 2), which are not already well managed, and so tend to be one-offs. But independent studies have shown average savings from e-auction repetitions, of 11–15 per cent, in both Europe and the United States. The companies engaged in enabling e-commerce will obviously tend to highlight the cases with higher savings, so expectations may need to be managed.

The power of e-commerce software has increased in recent years, and the price per auction event has fallen. Most companies could benefit from e-auctioning at least some of their spend areas. E-procurement is covered in Chapter 9.

Take account of the cost of the vendor's raw materials

One of my first efforts when I started in procurement in the mid-1980s was to seek a price reduction from BP, for the bulk polyethylene they supplied my company. There had been major falls, in the preceding weeks, in the price of crude oil on world markets. Knowing that plastics were ultimately derived from crude oil, I figured that a price reduction was due. The salesman pointed out that the two markets were quite different, with their own supply and demand characteristics, so he couldn't reduce the price of polyethylene for me. But I persisted, and he came out with a great line I'm sure he used every day with uppity people like me. Did I want him to put me in touch with a colleague on the crude oil selling side of BP, who could sell me some oil at prices lower than they had been for some time? The implication was that I could then convert it into polyethylene myself.

In the case of many goods, there is a clear relationship between the full cost of production and the cost of input raw materials. It may be worthwhile – and will certainly reduce administrative efforts – if a formula can be worked out so that the cost of goods may be varied at regular intervals, in line with independent cost indices. The reason this is important in the context of cost reduction is that in the absence of such a mechanism, vendors are likely to raise your prices when the costs of raw materials rise, but not reduce your prices when the costs of raw materials fall – the so-called 'ratchet effect'.

An example of buyers routinely relating cost prices to vendors' raw material prices is the carrier bags bought by retailers from the Far East. Now the buyer will know the weight of the prime raw material (low-density polyethylene – LDPE) in the bags. He can see the 'spot price' for LDPE in the Far East from independent market pricing indices. Two of the most widely used providers of such information are: Platts Polymerscan (www.platts.com); and Independent Chemical Information Services – London Oil Reports, thankfully abbreviated to ICIS-LOR (www.icis.com).

Combining the weight of the carrier bag with the spot price of LDPE, the buyer is in a position to estimate the LDPE cost within each bag. On a periodic basis, as specified in the contract – probably monthly or quarterly – the price of the bags will be adjusted in line with the price index for LDPE.

It is quite feasible to 'share the gain' and 'share the pain' of raw material price movements. One obvious way would be to 'fix' a raw material price on a given date, maybe the contract start date, and then only adjust the purchase price to take account of a proportion – 50 per cent say – of the actual raw material prices movement, against the fixed price. Include two or three worked examples in the contract, to guard against the possibility of misunderstanding.

Take account of exchange rates

If you are buying from overseas vendors, operating a different currency to your own, you may have to (or wish to) take account of exchange rates – even if you are buying those goods or services in your own currency.

There is always the possibility that exchange rates at the time of ordering, and at the time of invoice settlement, will be different. Now your bank will take you through options designed to reduce your risk, but you could alternatively have an exchange rate clause in your contract. Again, be sure to include two or three worked examples in the contract.

Worked examples

Let's say a UK-based buyer orders an item of capital equipment from a vendor based in the United States, at a cost of £100,000, and the exchange rate at the time of ordering is £1.00 = US $2.00. The contract requires the buyer to pay for the item 30 days after receipt, in sterling. The contract has an exchange rate fluctuation mechanism, to the effect that the sterling price will remain unchanged, when the exchange rate on the date of invoice settlement varies from the exchange rate on the date of ordering, by less than 2.5 per cent. The same term also states that where the exchange rate varies by 2.5 per cent or more, the difference against the 2.5 per cent point will be used to adjust the sterling price payable by the buyer.

Worked example 1: The exchange rate on the date of invoice settlement is £1.00 = £2.04. This is within the 2.5% band, so the buyer pays £100,000.

Worked example 2: The exchange rate on the date of invoice settlement is £1.00 = US $1.90. This is 5% less than the exchange rate at the time of ordering, so the UK buyer will have to pay a higher sterling price, 5.0% – 2.5% = 2.5% higher, or £102,500.

Worked example 3: The exchange rate on the date of invoice settlement is £1.00 = US $2.08. This is 4% higher than the exchange rate at the time of ordering, so the UK buyer will have to pay a lower sterling price, 4.0% – 2.5% = 1.5% lower, or £98,500.

Ensure vendors are delivering their contractual commitments

After negotiating a complex contract, a buyer's attention may well turn elsewhere – however, it's important that contracts are actively managed, and time set aside for this activity. For some contracts, this will include checking that invoice pricing is in line with the contract, and that retrospective rebates are not only properly calculated, but actually received.

From time to time, I come across situations where a vendor is overcharging against an existing contract, or is in breach of contract in other ways. The potential cost savings from such situations can be significant, as can be seen in the following case study.

CASE STUDY: AN ELECTRICITY COMPANY REDUCES ITS CHARGES, AND REFUNDS ITS CUSTOMER A TOTAL OF £446,000

Company: Retailer
Spend area: Electricity
Annual spend: £2.6 million
Summary: £446,000 savings were secured for the client.

Background

In the late summer of 2001, a regional electricity company (REC) proposed a new two-year contract to my client, rather than the more customary one-year contract. I advised my client to decline the proposal, whereupon the REC improved its offer by £66,000. I advised my client to decline the new proposal, but the company committed to it anyway.

My client had historically not carried out proactive management in the area of electricity, and no mechanisms were in place to check the accuracy of billing data.

Wholesale electricity prices fell after October 2001, thereby making the new two-year contract uncompetitive, giving the client an incentive to terminate the contract early. However, the client was unaware of any grounds on which it might terminate the contract.

Action taken

I carried out comparisons of the new and old supply agreement prices, against invoices received from the REC. This exercise revealed extensive historical mis-billing, and eventually led to refunds of £260,000 over the course of some months.

This still left the matter of the new agreement being uncompetitive. I examined the contract in detail, and noted a clause to the effect that if a breach of contract were not rectified within seven days, my client would have the right to terminate the contract early. The REC was unable to rectify the breach (the mis-billing) within the required time, so my client was able to threaten early termination. I negotiated a rebate of £120,000, in return for our client agreeing to continue obtaining electricity from the REC for the remainder of the contract.

Outcome

Cash savings of £446,000 had resulted from my involvement, a process put in place to validate bill accuracy, and preparations made for a robust tender process to be executed in the spring/summer of 2003.

CHANGE *WHEN* IT IS BOUGHT

Defer expenditure

Private sector companies are as prone as public sector organizations to spending money allocated within budgets, for fear it will be withdrawn in the subsequent budget period. The consequences can be ill-advised buying decisions.

Consignment stocking

The vendor can finance stock in the buyer's plant, and the buyer only pays for it once used. This helps avert stock shortages and assists cash flow.

CHANGE *WHO* BUYS IT

Develop or support managers

Few budget-holders have substantial buying expertise, although many think they do. For companies that are serious about reducing their costs, there will generally be a need for staff competence development, through two routes: 1) external courses, such as those run through the Chartered Institute of Purchasing and Supply (CIPS) – see Appendix 3; 2) exposure to external experts, whether interim managers or consultants.

Use external experts

The use of interim managers and consultants is covered in Chapter 10. They can, of course, be used to negotiate contracts on your behalf, and train your staff to manage the contracts when they leave. Alternatively, they can work on a part-time basis over the medium to longer term. This can be a highly cost-effective approach for the company, and it means the experts are less likely to become 'stale' over time.

Ensure an appropriate organizational structure for buying

The case for a professional buying function can be obvious even in small companies, but unfortunately small companies tend not to be attractive to procurement professionals. There has long been a shortage of truly proficient professionals, and they tend to be attracted by the variety and rewards of working in large companies, or they work as interim managers or consultants.

Where decision making is devolved over a number of sites, the extent of centralization/decentralization needs to be considered in detail. The issue of organizational structures for buying is considered at length in Chapter 10.

CHANGE *WHERE* YOU BUY IT FROM

Vendor base reduction

When executed properly, vendor base reduction should result in cost improvements, because the available demand is spread between fewer vendors – but a market-testing process will probably be required to seize the available savings.

Buying from overseas vendors

Overseas vendors can be a source of considerable cost reduction potential, and the topic is covered in Chapter 5.

Shorten the supply chain

Opportunities may exist to reduce the supply chain, eg buying directly from manufacturers rather than from wholesalers.

RENT RATHER THAN BUY?

Some organizations are wedded to the idea of buying items of capital equipment – forklift trucks, say – while a little effort and imagination might reveal the benefits of renting the equipment. The organization might then be in a position to benefit from superior equipment, as I will explain shortly.

To illustrate the point, let's say an organization needs to acquire 10 new forklift trucks and, after some market testing, has identified the lowest-cost option, while still providing it with equipment of adequate specification. The trucks have a combined purchase price of £100,000, and an economic working life of five years. A comprehensive mainte-nance package for all the trucks will cost £10,000 pa.

Now the organization could buy the trucks outright, account for depreciation in the usual way, and hope to sell them for a token sum at the end of the period. Or it could carry out a market-testing exercise where it sought costs for both outright purchase and rental options, along with a defined maintenance package.

And this is where matters become more interesting – because the trucks with the lowest purchase price might not be the trucks with the lowest rental costs. Indeed, the organization may well find that if it were to rent rather than buy the trucks, it could afford to buy superior equipment to that which it would have selected on the basis of purchase price alone. This is important, but counter-intuitive, so it's important that I explain the phenomenon.

Equipment manufacturers differ markedly in the extent of their equipment's depreciation over time. I use the term 'depreciation' here not in a financial accounting sense, but in the sense of equipment's market value over time. Some manufacturers' build quality, reputation, or expertise at obtaining good prices for used equipment is such that their equipment depreciates more slowly than other manufacturers' equipment. To use a term we're more familiar with in respect of the cars we acquire for our personal use, their residual values are higher.

By carrying out a market-testing exercise, and seeking both purchase prices and rental costs, as well as maintenance costs, you are effectively applying competitive pressure to a number of elements:

- the outright purchase price;
- the residual value – because if you go for the rental option you are financing not the outright purchase price, but the purchase price less the residual value;
- the interest rate for the financing sum involved – and some manufacturers may well have access to lower interest rates than you could access, and competitive pressure forces them to share at least part of that benefit with you;
- the maintenance package – the manufacturer will need to maintain the equipment in a good condition, not only to retain your goodwill and improve their prospect for landing future contracts, but also to maximize the residual value at the end of the rental term, and therefore their financial return from the contract.

To illustrate the point about residual values, let's consider a worked example, Table 4.1. To keep things simple, I've left interest out of the example. The example assumes two different vendors, the first at the 'economy' end of the market, the second at the 'prestige' end, with a strong reputation for equipment reliability, repair speediness, and more besides.

Table 4.1 The impact of residual values on rental costs

Purchase price (£) = A	Residual value after 5 years (£) = B	Sum to be financed over 5 years (£) = C = A – B	Quarterly rental costs (£) = C/20
100,000	10,000	90,000	4,500
120,000	40,000	80,000	4,000

So if you were to make a vendor selection on the basis of purchase price, you would probably opt for the first vendor. But if you were to make the selection on the basis of rental costs, you would opt for the second. And the second vendor would probably give you better contract performance, because good reputations – in commerce as elsewhere – are not gained overnight, and they need to be constantly protected.

INVOLVE PROCUREMENT AT AN EARLIER STAGE IN THE BUYING CYCLE

If you have a proficient buying team, it may well be worth involving them in the buying cycle somewhat earlier than you might normally. Buyers often complain – and with good reason – that they are brought into projects at a late stage, after the specification of a good or service has been established and a preferred vendor selected, and they are then expected to negotiate a significant cost reduction, usually under great time pressure. Now it is sometimes possible to achieve some improvement, but it is a poor way of operating.

The later in the buying cycle (Chapter 3) the buyer is involved, the less is the scope for cost reduction, as illustrated in Figure 4.1.

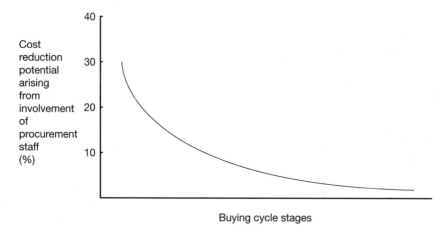

Figure 4.1   *The decline in cost reduction potential over the buying cycle*

This phenomenon can largely be explained by the fact that the buying cycle is not a familiar concept outside the buying community, in particular the importance of the first four stages:

1.   Define the objectives.
2.   Define organizational requirements.

3.   Define information needs, and develop a project plan.
4.   Undertake market research.

Now these stages should provide the buyer with at least a number of viable potential vendors. And this alone will be enough to bring competitive pressure to bear on price levels.

5

Market testing

There are two ways to identify the lowest price obtainable: guess, or market test. Don't guess.

(Andrew Heslop, procurement consultant, 2007)

This chapter contains:

- Why market testing is so important.
- Different types of market testing.
- Locating potential new vendors.
- Buying internationally.
- Market testing in difficult markets.
- Case studies.

WHY MARKET TESTING IS SO IMPORTANT

Market testing is the process at the heart of most successful cost reduction initiatives. It provides an opportunity for a number of viable new vendors to gain a new customer, something that is obviously important to them. It follows that the current vendor(s) may lose the business. The current vendors' best hope may be to retain the business – or some of it –

but usually with lower margins, due to the competitive forces unleashed by the market-testing process.

That's the very reason why incumbent vendors will do all within their power to prevent market testing being carried out, once they've 'caught wind' of its possibility, and will typically use some or all of the following tactics:

- They will portray the buyer, and the buyer's company, as 'disloyal', and unappreciative of their historical contribution to the company.
- They will intimate that the thinking behind market testing is unsophisticated at best, and crude at worst.
- They will portray a decision to switch to another vendor as being risky, and will have a range of anecdotes describing the terrible outcomes that befell other customers who had the temerity to switch – 'they came back to us a month a later, the service from the new vendor was so bad!' being a particular favourite.
- If all else fails, they may offer a price reduction to the buyer in an effort to discourage the market-testing exercise, often suggesting that the buyer will look good in the eyes of his bosses, and he can then spend his time more profitably looking at other spend areas. But the buyer can be sure that any price reductions offered voluntarily, however substantial, will be markedly lower than the price reductions the same vendor would be prepared to offer during a market-testing exercise.

In the 1980s, when the core business of the IBM Corporation was manufacturing and selling computer hardware, IBM sales executives were taught the mantra, 'No IT director ever got fired for choosing IBM'. One can only speculate how many IT directors paid an extra x per cent for IBM hardware, rather than their competitors' hardware, to help them sleep at night.

Once a market-testing exercise is under way, the vendors – both the incumbents and potential new ones – may try to corrupt the decision-making process, through a number of tactics, mostly focusing on the 'decision-making unit' for vendor selection. The decision-making unit consists of the executives who have any influence on the vendor selection process, often including operational or technical staff. It is critical that the buyer and his colleagues are clear about their respective roles, responsibilities and authorities, with respect to the market-testing exercise. Managing information flows will be a particularly important matter.

I am often astonished at the reluctance of companies to conduct market-testing exercises. Very often this is the result of one or more of the 'unhelpful mindsets' outlined in Chapter 1, but also sometimes the result of sheer laziness. A proficient market-testing exercise takes time and effort, and some executives are simply not motivated to carry them out – they prefer an easy life, dealing with the vendors they've always dealt with.

The frequency with which market testing is carried out is increasing over time, partly because more and more companies are realizing the benefits that flow from it, and partly because companies are increasingly turning to e-procurement (Chapter 9) and international buying (covered later in this chapter) to reduce their costs.

DIFFERENT TYPES OF MARKET TESTING

Market testing is sometimes referred to as 'tendering', but this can be misleading. Strictly speaking, tendering is the process whereby a buying organization outlines the goods and/or services it requires, and a number of companies then 'tender' for the business, ie they make a formal offer which the buying organization may or may not accept, thereby creating a contract.

The real world is often more complicated. The buying organization may be uncertain about a number of matters, and asking a number of questions, most notably:

- Who are the viable vendors in this market? Are they financially secure?
- Should we consider using local/national/regional/overseas vendors?
- Should we consider an e-procurement solution?
- What is the range of possible solutions to our need?
- What contract terms would be appropriate for this spend area?
- How might we develop a specification or service level agreement that would be unambiguous, so we can consider rival bids as directly comparable?
- We've defined exactly what we want, we know the marketplace and the range of vendors we wish to tender for our business, so how might we best obtain the maximum value for money?

It may be the case that your prime cost reduction opportunities are spend areas where you are perceived within the supply marketplace as an important customer, and over time the most competitive vendors will seek to meet with you. But equally, this may not be the case, particularly if your company is not a large business of a particular class or service. Your prime cost reduction opportunities may lie in areas where you are still not significant in the marketplace, and you will need to carry out some market research. An example is provided in the following case study.

CASE STUDY: A BUYER MANAGED FOR 20 YEARS TO BE UNAWARE OF THE EXISTENCE OF THE LEADING VENDOR IN A MARKET

In the course of a cost reduction assignment at a medium-sized retailer, I met a manager whose span of responsibilities included the buying of printed carrier bags for his company. He was said to have lengthy negotiations with the various vendors, and he'd been buying carrier bags for 20 years. His boss had expressed his satisfaction with this area, and saw the manager as a tough negotiator. To substantiate this, the boss cited the manager halving cost increase demands sought by vendors to compensate for rising prices for polyethylene (the prime raw material in carrier bags) in the Far East, where the bags were manufactured.

In the course of a brief conversation, however, it became clear to me that the manager knew little about the marketplace for carrier bags, or the various issues that might influence the prices over time. I carried out some market research, and soon identified the leading vendor in the market, which supplied most of the major retailers and could be expected to enjoy significant economies of scale. The vendor was some 10 times larger than the vendors from whom my client had been buying for 20 years.

My client's manager had never even heard of this vendor. It turned out that his approach to buying was entirely reactive, ie he would only meet with whichever vendors had made the effort to contact him. Meeting with numerous small vendors had kept him so busy that he had no time for market research. Even worse, he had no sense whatever of the need for market research.

A tender process resulted in a contract being awarded to the new vendor, and the outcome was very successful – bag quality was improved, and a 25 per cent cost reduction achieved. A simple formula was developed to adjust bag prices in line with the impact of Far Eastern polyethylene cost movements (reductions as well as increases), based on the polyethylene content of each bag.

So, what are the different possible approaches to market testing? The most commonly used ones are outlined in Table 5.1, along with details of the scenarios in which they're used.

A template for an RFP is provided in Appendix 2, to help you develop documents of your own. An electronic version may be downloaded from www.lpsconsulting.co.uk.

It is important to realize that the market-testing types are not mutually exclusive. So – by way of example – you might execute an RFI process to establish which vendors were viable in some way(s), and therefore to be considered potential vendors for an RFQ.

Table 5.1   Different approaches to market testing, and when used

Market testing type	When used
RFI (request for information)	You require information on the marketplace, specifications and service level agreements, vendors' capabilities, financial standing...
RFP (request for proposal)	You have a rough idea of what you want to achieve, but are unsure of the options available to achieve it.
RFQ (request for quotation)	You have a clear specification or service level agreement, and need to ask potential vendors to quote for supplying the good or service.
ITT (invitation to tender)	You have a clear specification or service level agreement, and want to ask potential vendors to put forward an offer, which you will be able to accept, and a formal contract result.

LOCATING POTENTIAL NEW VENDORS

There are numerous approaches to locating potential new vendors, the following being the most viable.

Trade fairs

If you can't manage to attend the relevant trade fair, ask the event organizer for a list of exhibitors – an instant potential supplier list.

Buying internationally

Guidance on locating potential overseas vendors is provided in the next section.

Professional bodies

Professional bodies for individual market sectors will be able to provide a list of members able to satisfy your requirements.

Networking

If you mix with executives buying from the same market sector of interest as you, you should be able to obtain good tips on viable vendors, and more besides.

E-procurement enablers

A number of e-procurement enablers have built up large lists of potential vendors, which they can make available. Vendors are increasingly seeing the value of being on such lists.

Sourcing guides

Three of the most commonly used guides in the UK are those available from Kompass (www.kompass.co.uk), Kelly's (www.kellysearch.co.uk) and Yellow Pages (www.yell.com). They have different offerings, so you will need to see which best meets your needs. Kelly's claim the following scope:

- 2,000,000 companies;
- 200,000 product categories;
- 200 countries, across 5 continents.

Very round numbers, I think you'll agree. Some of the information providers offer added-value services such as financial reports on vendors, usually for a small fee.

Internet searches

My own experience of trying to locate vendors through internet searches – using key words – has been very frustrating, often leading to hundreds or even thousands of potential vendors. And often the largest vendors in a marketplace aren't among those sponsoring a link. But I do know other procurement professionals who find internet searching a useful approach, especially in marketplaces where there are only a few potential vendors.

BUYING INTERNATIONALLY

The case for buying internationally

For many organizations, the case for buying internationally may be compelling. For buyers in the UK, there may well be cost reduction opportunities with vendors based elsewhere in the European Union, particularly given the decline of the UK's manufacturing sector over a long period. At least these buyers will not need to pay import duties from other EU countries.

For many buyers, opportunities lie in low-cost country sourcing (LCCS). Some major organizations have people devoted full-time to the task of LCCS. The reasons are obvious. Manufacturers and service providers in many developing countries have low labour and material costs compared with more developed economies, often throughout their supply chains. Buying internationally clearly takes more of an effort than buying from vendors within one's own country of operation, and there are numerous risks and difficulties involved. But they are not insurmountable.

Developing competence in buying internationally

Given the opportunities and risks inherent in buying internationally, I would recommend to anyone interested in the subject that they initially attend a course on the subject. Alan Bracken, a Logistics Consultant with ABTS Logistics (www.abtslogistics.co.uk), runs an excellent two-day course through CIPS, covering:

- methods of sourcing;
- identifying your cost centres;
- purchasing under Incoterms 2000;
- import licences;
- tariff quotas;
- Preferential Trading Agreements;
- understanding the Tariff Book;
- the role of shipping documents in international purchasing;
- Bills of Lading;
- Master and House Air Waybill;
- Insurance Certificates;
- identifying the most effective mode of transport (sea, land or air);
- costing for freight;

- planning for profit – Duty and VAT Deferment, Inward Processing Relief (IPR), bonded warehousing, rejected orders and repayment of duty and VAT;
- methods of payment and related costs – establishing a Letter of Credit, preparing Bills of Exchange, Cash against Documents;
- pre-delivery inspection facilities;
- customs clearance.

The material in the remainder of this section is drawn from the CIPS course.

Incoterms

There are often a number of independent organizations involved in transporting goods by sea or air, and this raises issues of risk, insurance, costs, and more. The problem is exacerbated by the existence of different business cultures around the world, and different languages.

Following a long period of confusion over terminology, which had resulted in numerous disputes, the International Chamber of Commerce was approached in the 1930s to devise standard terms for goods transportation internationally. The outcome was the publication of the first International Commercial Terms guide in 1936 – 'Incoterms 1936'. The document has since been revised a number of times, the latest being in 2000 – 'Incoterms 2000' – and it is expected to remain valid for some years to come. It can be purchased through Chambers of Commerce.

Incoterms 2000 defines three basic elements:

- place – where the seller delivers the goods to the buyer;
- cost – what the buyer pays for, up to the point of delivery;
- risk – where the seller passes the transit risk to the buyer.

It is important that buyers make clear in writing when they are seeking quotations from vendors, and subsequently ordering from them, that they are contracting under Incoterms, and exactly which term. Table 5.2 outlines appropriate Incoterm options for different modes of transport.

A word of warning at this point. The buyer needs to be very careful about the detail behind the terms. A good example is CIF. The seller is obliged under Incoterms to take out at least a minimum level of insurance, termed 'Institute Cargo Clauses (C)'. The 'Institute' in this case is the Institute of London Underwriters. But there are also 'A' and 'B' versions, which give superior cover, for higher premiums. The point is that the buyer should not assume that the insurance included in CIF is necessarily adequate for their purposes.

Table 5.2   Incoterm abbreviations and their meanings

Incoterm abbreviation	Meanings
Any mode of transport, including multimodal	
EXW	EX-Works (named place)
FCA	Free Carrier (named place)
CPT	Carriage Paid To (named place)
CIP	Carriage and Insurance Paid to (named place)
DAF	Delivered At Frontier (named place)
DDP	Delivered Duty Paid (named place)
DDU	Delivered Duty Unpaid (named place)
Inland waterway transport	
CFR	Cost and Freight (named port of destination)
CIF	Cost, Insurance and Freight (named port of destination)
DES	Delivered Ex Ship (named port of destination)
DEQ	Delivered Ex Quay (named port of destination)

Identifying potential vendors

A key question facing buyers is how to identify potential overseas vendors. Now some people appear to believe this problem has been solved by searches on the internet, but this simply isn't the case, except in rare cases. The following are the key practical options.

Embassies

Most of the countries worth considering – in terms of LCCS – have commercial sections in their London embassies. They will be able to assist with identifying potential vendors.

Chambers of Commerce

The International Chamber of Commerce (www.iccwbo.org) is worth approaching, in order to locate individual countries' Chambers of Commerce.

Trade fairs

It can be worth visiting trade fairs that focus on the spend areas you have in mind. Alternatively, to save the effort and cost of visiting, consider asking the event organizer for a list of exhibitors, along with their contact details.

Professional bodies

These are bodies representing particular industries, and it could be worth approaching the UK bodies and asking them for the contact details of the equivalent bodies overseas.

International sourcing guides

The guides most widely used by UK buyers are Kompass (www.kompass. co.uk) and Kelly Search (www.kellysearch.co.uk).

Department for Business, Enterprise and Regulatory Reform

The DBERR will supply contact details for British Embassies overseas, which will have details of vendors in their countries.

Commercial agencies/buying agents

These organizations locate viable vendors for a fee.

Quality assurance

Buyers starting to source internationally have concerns about quality of goods. But assuming they have carried out due diligence in their vendor selection, this should not be a problem. However, in recognition of the issue, a number of organizations have evolved to carry out pre-shipment inspections (PSIs). They carry out inspections and test in line with guidelines put forward by the buyer, for example on sampling frequency. After inspecting and approving goods, they can seal containers with their own seal, to protect against the risk that the vendor substitutes inferior goods post-inspection.

A Swiss-based firm, Société Générale de Surveillance (SGS), is the world's leading inspection, verification, testing and certification company. They have over 1,000 offices and laboratories, and more than 48,000 employees around the world. Details may be found on www.sgs.com.

MARKET TESTING IN DIFFICULT MARKETS

There are a number of markets where most organizations struggle to effectively market test, due to one or more of the following reasons:

- technical complexity of the good or service;
- difficulty in analysing demand to the detailed level required;
- a complex supply market, possibly with some major risks;
- inadequate buyer experience, expertise or time;
- insufficient spend to warrant lengthy buyer attention.

In many cases, the company may only need to market test on a periodic basis – every year or two, say – and it clearly wouldn't make sense for a company to have full-time employees with the required experience and expertise.

For most organizations, a number of utilities – including electricity – fit into the 'difficult to market test' category, and for this very reason, independent organizations have emerged to provide a practical solution. One such is the UK's Energy Information Centre, EIC (www.eic.co.uk), founded in 1975. I've used them a number of times over the years, and can highly recommend them. EIC is the UK's leading independent consultancy for industrial, commercial and public-sector energy users. They cover the electricity, gas, water and oil industries, providing wholesale and retail market intelligence, outsourced procurement and accounting solutions, energy management services, and a consultancy service to develop clients' energy strategies.

One of the reasons I used EIC was that they had – and still have – a stated policy of not accepting commissions from the energy providers that they recommend to clients. A number of other consultancies adopt the same position. EIC's position in their marketplace is such that their reputation would be severely damaged should they be known to accept such commissions. The importance of this issue struck me a few years ago, when I was negotiating a new electricity contract for a client. The incumbent energy supplier enquired if they needed to pay a commission to me, 'like we did to the last consultant'. It emerged that the consultant who had negotiated the existing contract had received not only a commission from my client, but also one from the energy company, which he had not declared to my client – a clear conflict of interest, and I politely declined the energy supplier's offer. My preference is always to pay a flat fee to the consultancy involved, rather than be tempted into 'sharing savings' schemes.

Another approach to buying in 'difficult markets' is to periodically attend specialist courses, which can be a very cost-effective way to 'get up to speed'. In 2007/08, CIPS are running a number of courses of such a nature:

- Fundamentals of Buying Telecommunications.
- Buying Business Travel.
- The Procurement of Specialist Contract and Temporary Workers.
- Buying Legal Services.
- Buying Security Services.
- Buying Corporate Wear – defining your brand and image.
- Energy – Commodity Buying in a Volatile Environment.
- The Fundamentals of Buying and Managing Consultants.
- The Principles of Buying Distribution Services.
- Buying Catering Services.
- The Insider's Guide to Agencies.
- An Introductory Seminar on Buying Advertising.
- Understanding and Buying Design.
- Understanding IT Procurement.
- A Commercial Approach to Data Protection in Procurement.
- A Commercial Approach to Software Agreements.
- Purchasing Matters – Software Licensing.
- IT Disputes – Clearing up the Mess.
- A Commercial Approach to IP in Procurement.

CASE STUDIES

The following three case studies are provided to give you a flavour of the potential benefits of market testing. They cover three goods and services, which I market tested for a UK professional services firm.

CASE STUDY: MARKET TESTING STATIONERY AND PRINT SAVES A CLIENT £1.5 MILLION OVER THREE YEARS

Company: UK professional services firm
Spend area: Stationery and print (eg letterheads)
Annual spend: £1.27 million
Summary: In excess of £500,000 pa (39 per cent) overall cost savings were forecast, or £1.5m over the three-year contract term. Much-improved contractual terms were negotiated.

Background

Like all professional service firms, my client was a major user of office stationery and printed materials. The firm was quite convinced that it was obtaining excellent value for money from its longstanding vendor, as a facilities manager had conducted a market-testing exercise the previous year. But I was not persuaded of the rigour of that exercise, so I carried out my own investigations, and discovered:

- onerous contractual terms (the vendor's own);
- poor contract management by the client;
- no understanding of material specifications, nor the specification changes which could lead to reduced pricing;
- lack of performance measurement data;
- highly competitive marketplace, with one major vendor very keen to break into the sector.

Action taken

I implemented a two-phase approach: 1) internal discussions to explore which specification changes might be acceptable to the firm; 2) a request for proposal (RFP) was sent to the incumbent vendor, and two leading competitors.

Outcome

Following lengthy negotiations, the incumbent vendor was retained. Fierce competition, along with numerous specification changes, led to an overall cost saving of £500,000 pa, or £1.5m over the new three-year contract period. Contractual terms were greatly improved, including new performance measures and the provision of detailed management information.

CASE STUDY: MARKET TESTING ARCHIVING SERVICES SAVES A CLIENT £120,000 PA

Company: UK professional services firm
Spend area: Archiving services
Annual spend: £590,000
Summary: In excess of £120,000 pa (20 per cent) overall cost savings were forecast, with some vendor changes, and much improved contractual terms.

Background

Like many professional service firms, my client occupied high-cost premises, and generated a great deal of paperwork, which often needed to be stored for many years – sometimes indefinitely. Document scanning was not a cost-effective alternative option. The client had amassed a great deal of data on this area, but had failed to devise a viable strategy. I was asked to investigate and recommend a strategy, and discovered:

- no senior-level interest in, nor management of, this area;
- client's materials stored in nine warehouses, operated by four vendors;
- a wide variety of charging mechanisms in place;
- only one valid contract in place – others had 'run on';
- highly competitive marketplace in most geographical areas, but permanent withdrawal charges discouraged inter-vendor material transfers.

I recommended a market-testing exercise be carried out forthwith, with a view to reducing costs. The client agreed, and asked me to conduct the exercise through to final contract negotiation.

Action taken

A request for proposal (RFP) was issued, with associated contractual terms, and sent to existing and potential vendors. The documentation included a much-simplified charging mechanism for storage and movements.

Outcome

Three of the four vendors dropped storage charges markedly, so as to discourage transfers. The materials within the fourth vendor were transferred to a competitor, which paid the associated transport costs. Overall savings in excess of £120,000 pa (20 per cent) were forecast.

CASE STUDY: MARKET TESTING PHOTOCOPIERS SAVES A CLIENT £400,000 OVER FOUR YEARS

Company: UK professional services firm
Spend area: Photocopiers
Annual spend: £450,000
Summary: In excess of £100,000 pa (22 per cent) overall cost savings were delivered, with the introduction of new equipment under much-improved contractual terms.

Background

Like all professional service firms, our client was dependent upon efficient document management, in which copiers play a significant role. Following complaints about poor equipment reliability, I was asked to investigate and recommend a strategy, and discovered:

- 73 items of equipment across the estate, including some high-speed copiers for print rooms, and a small number of colour copiers;
- eight providers of equipment and associated maintenance services;
- no effective management of this area at either a central or local level;
- all copiers purchased four or more years ago, or leases expired;
- poor equipment reliability due to a combination of general wear and tear, and a lack of contract terms to ensure high equipment uptime.

I recommended a data-gathering and market-testing exercise be carried out forthwith, with a view to replacing all equipment. The client agreed, and asked me to conduct the exercise through to final contract negotiation.

Action taken

Data gathering and analysis took place over a period of four weeks, followed by a request for proposal (RFP), with associated robust contractual terms, being sent to major manufacturers/resellers and maintenance providers. Machine assessments were carried out.

Outcome

The most attractive bid was received from a reseller which already enjoyed a strong reputation with the client, and could supply equipment from the leading manufacturer in the market. The contract terms were accepted by the vendor in full, which gave confidence that equipment uptime levels would be high over the four-year contract term. Savings of £100,000 pa were delivered.

6

Outsourcing and insourcing

Outsourcing is a growing phenomenon, but it's something that we should realize is probably a plus for the economy in the long run. It's just a new way of doing international trade.

(2004 Economic Report of the President, Gregory Mankiw, chairman of the White House Council of Economic Advisors)

This chapter contains:

- Background.
- Deciding what to outsource.
- Levels of outsourcing.
- The top three legal issues.
- Insourcing.

BACKGROUND

The term 'outsourcing' denotes the act of transferring services or manufacturing activities, which the organization previously performed 'in-house', ie with its own employees, to one or more external organizations. For some years the most important objective has been cost reduction, but we shall see that organizations are increasingly seeing opportunities to meet other objectives.

The term 'insourcing' denotes the opposite, ie starting to perform in-house that which was previously performed by external organizations. The area might – or might not – have been performed in-house at some point in the buying organization's history.

DECIDING WHAT TO OUTSOURCE

While cost reduction is a key driver behind many outsourcing drives, there are sometimes a wide range of other issues to be considered, and ideally measured, when deciding whether or not to outsource services or manufacturing. The principal ones are outlined in Table 6.1.

Table 6.1   Key considerations to be taken into account, in deciding whether or not to outsource manufacturing or services

Considerations	Questions to be answered
Financial	What is the expected price competitiveness of the two options, now and into the future?
	Will there be enough capital available to fund the necessary ongoing investment for an in-house operation?
	Are there enough adequately qualified staff, now and into the future?
	Is demand highly uncertain, leading to concern over the economic viability of an in-house operation?
	Does the in-house operation make a useful contribution to wider company overheads?
	What are the opportunity costs of an in-house operation, eg could the area in the plant or office be put to more productive use?
	Of what value would be the reduction in inventory and obsolescence resulting from buying?
Customer service	Which option would improve customer service, eg can we offer customers shorter lead-times with an in-house operation?
Confidentiality	Do we need to maintain a high level of secrecy, to the point that we would not wish to outsource this, regardless of financial or other considerations?
Quality	What quality issues need to be addressed?
Innovation	Can we expect vendors to deliver innovation over time, which we could not expect our own staff to deliver?

Michael Corbett is a recognized authority on the subject of outsourcing theory and practice, and his book (Corbett, 2004) is strongly recommended to readers interested in the subject. At the 2004 World Outsourcing Summit, which Corbett's firm produced, respondents provided the following top eight reasons for outsourcing:

- cost reduction (49%);
- focus improvement (17%);
- improvement to variability of cost structure (12%);
- access to skills (9%);
- revenue growth (4%);
- quality improvement (3%);
- capital conversation (3%);
- innovation (3%).

The book explains how to:

- determine the value of outsourcing for any business process;
- analyse the risks, evaluate their potential impact, and use a range of techniques to reduce, eliminate and manage them;
- identify, evaluate and select the right partner(s);
- turn contractor relationships into long-term, successful outsourcing relationships;
- transition people, processes and technologies to the outsourcing state;
- identify, develop and reward outsourcing managers;
- create new ways of doing business, ahead of the competition.

The issue of whether or not to outsource some or all of a company's manufacturing operations is known as the 'make or buy' question. It also extends to the possibility of outsourcing some in-house support areas, which produce physical goods for the company, such as print operations or high-volume photocopying operations.

After they have outsourced a service, buyers tend to have exaggerated expectations of the extent to which vendors will pass on the benefit of any cost reductions they have experienced. For this reason, buyers need to 'keep in touch' periodically with the supply market, to ensure costs at the chosen vendor have not become out of line with the market.

LEVELS OF OUTSOURCING

At the time of writing (November 2007), the bestselling book at Amazon on the topic of outsourcing is one written by two writers based in the United States (Brown and Wilson, 2005). _The Black Book of Outsourcing_ is a 'must-read' for anyone with a serious interest in the topic. It provides some startling data and commentary on the extent and fast growth rate of outsourcing activities, particularly with reference to the United States and the United Kingdom.

It presents a lucid explanation of the potential contribution of outsourcing to corporate objectives, and national economies. One striking subject is the rapid extension of outsourcing into functional areas long assumed to be immune. A few sentences from the book's Introduction might raise concern among some executives, with respect to their own futures:

> We have to face facts: most of the white-collar and executive jobs downsized in the last few years in the United States and the United Kingdom are gone forever... The hard truth is that the rules that used to guide us in shaping a career, starting a new business, or leading an established company, no longer apply. The complexities of outsourcing are forcing drastic managerial and professional career changes...

The authors make interesting distinctions between three 'levels' of outsourcing:

Tactical outsourcing
The firm is already in trouble, and outsourcing is seen as a direct way to address some of their problems. So tactical relationships are forged to:

- Generate immediate cost savings;
- Eliminate the need for future investments;
- Realize a cash infusion from the sale of assets;
- Relieve the burden of staffing.

Strategic outsourcing
Strategic outsourcing relationships are about building long-term value... corporations work with a smaller number of best-in-class integrated service providers.

Transformational outsourcing
Transformational outsourcing is third-generation outsourcing.... Those who take advantage of transformational outsourcing recognize that the real power of this tool lies in the innovations that outside specialists bring to their customers' businesses. No longer

are outsourcing service providers viewed only as tools for becoming more efficient or better focused; rather, they are seen as powerful forces for change – allies in the battle for market and mind share.

THE TOP THREE LEGAL ISSUES

When outsourcing, it is imperative that legal considerations are taken fully into account. In the UK, Pinsent Masons – a major law firm, and part of PMLG, an international group of law firms – has a high reputation in this area (as it does in many areas). I am indebted to Belinda Bell, a Senior Associate with the firm, for the remainder of the material in this section. Please note that this is intended as a high-level overview of some of the main issues that tend to arise in outsourcing transactions. It does not attempt to cover all the issues, and it is strongly recommended that specific legal advice be sought at the earliest stages of any outsourcing.

Outsourcing is very often described as a 'partnership' or 'joint venture', but in legal terms, it is usually neither of those things. An outsourcing arrangement is most often established by a network of contracts, the central contract being that for the provision of the services by the vendor, and supporting contracts, such as an asset and employee transfer agreement, a transitional agreement, project agreements, and potentially also a financial or parent company guarantee.

Although an exposition of the legal issues that must be considered in outsourcing transactions would run to a volume in itself, there are three key legal issues that seem to arise regardless of the nature of the services to be outsourced, or the industry in which the customer is involved. The three issues are:

- the very obvious, but often overlooked, need for contractual specificity and certainty as to what is being bought;
- the legal devices that can be used to limit and exclude (on the one hand) or reinforce (on the other hand) a party's responsibilities to another party;
- the 'people issues' associated with this sort of business change.

While by no means a 'recipe for success', early focus on these three key areas will provide a solid legal foundation for a good business outcome.

1. Services: scope and standard

The backbone of any outsourcing contract is the specification of the nature and extent of the services to be provided by the vendor. The production of a clear and detailed services description should be a joint commercial and legal objective. The commercial and technical focus must be on setting out, in business terms, what the customer is 'buying' (or expects to receive), and what the vendor is delivering. The legal focus must be to make sure that the contract describes all the 'hard' services (such as the provision of infrastructure) as well as the 'soft' services (such as attendance and participation in governance, and relationship steering activities).

It is also critical that the contract describes the agreed responsibility for interfaces – contractual interfaces (such as the interaction required with other vendors) and technical interfaces (including with the customer's own equipment). The language of this description must be contractual, and an essential element of contractual language is that it has to be sufficiently certain to be enforceable by the courts, so 'woolly' descriptions of the services, and sections which are simply transposed from requests for proposals and vendor responses, should be avoided.

In addition to a detailed description of the services, it is important from a legal perspective to assign actual, measurable quality standards to the key services. The customer will have difficulty complaining about 'poor standard' service if the required standard was not specified in the contract at the outset. Service quality is often defined by way of a set of service levels, which should be specific and measurable, and be linked to a contractual regime which encourages the vendor to meet those standards. The 'encouragement' can take the form of credits (against the charges), which accrue to the customer, if the required standard is not met. Legally, these should be drafted as an adjustment of the price payable, to reflect the decreased value of the service to the customer, rather than as a 'fine' or a 'penalty', which the courts would be unlikely to enforce. Service credits are generally useful for less serious breaches – those which would not entitle the customer to terminate the outsourcing contract – but it is a matter for negotiation whether this contractual remedy is the customer's exclusive remedy for such infractions, or whether a contractual or common law right to damages and/or termination will also apply.

Other useful legal devices to encourage good performance include liquidated damages provisions, where the point of reference should be the losses likely to be suffered by the customer. Agreeing liquidated damages ('liquidated' in this context simply means calculated and agreed up front, by way of a set figure, or method of reaching a set figure) can avoid the difficulty and expense of proving and assessing the actual loss caused by a vendor failure, such as failure to meet a transition timetable, or a service fault. It is important to bear in mind that liqui-dated damages are subject to some stringent legal rules, the most important of which is that they must represent a genuine pre-estimate of the customer's loss, or they will be held to be unenforceable.

2. Legal risk: liability and indemnities

As well as being careful to describe the services and service levels carefully, the parties to an outsourcing arrangement will (or should!) spend time assessing the business and financial risks associated with such a significant business change. Contractual apportionment of liability and the use of indemnities are two legal mechanisms available to deal with the risks which may be identified.

In an outsourcing context, making a decision on contractual apportionment of liability involves categorizing the particular types of risk and the likely resulting damage, and agreeing the exclusions and limitations on what compensation one party may recover from the other, if the particular circumstances arise. Where the contractual provisions setting up this apportionment are drafted carefully, they will bind the parties, and can override the right to recover according to common law principles.

The difficulty for a customer in this context is that the risks may be uncertain, and difficult to quantify. Vendors are usually very keen to limit the amount that a customer can recover, to some multiple of the value of the contract to the vendor, and this argument often seems to have a natural logic to it. While it is useful for a customer to know the vendor's 'risk/reward' calculation for negotiation purposes, from the customer's perspective, a contractual limit on liability should be set with regard to the likely losses a customer could sustain, rather than relating purely to the vendor's revenue stream.

As well as limitations on liability, parties to an outsourcing arrangement often negotiate exclusions of liability. In an outsourcing context, these are typically areas where the vendor is unwilling to accept any responsibility. The classic exclusion of liability which is commonplace in outsourcing contracts is an exclusion for so-called 'consequential' losses – which the lawyers will seek to define. Unsurprisingly, vendor lawyers generally seek to define this expression as widely as possible, as it is usually the vendor's liability that is at issue. Although it is reasonable in many circumstances to exclude genuinely indirect or remote losses, customers should be wary of agreeing to exclude all compensation for losing the expected cost savings and/or profit, as these are often the very benefits the customer is seeking to achieve by outsourcing!

On a brighter note, it has become commonplace for the parties to an outsourcing contract to agree between themselves particular areas where the vendor should be able to give the customer a guarantee of the vendor's 100 per cent responsibility. An indemnity is a legal device that is akin to a guarantee in this sense, and which can also facilitate the customer's route to claim. Savvy customers typically make sure that the vendor takes complete responsibility for the vendor's observance of the intellectual property rights of third parties in the provision of services, and they require an indemnity from the vendor should any of those third parties make an infringement claim against the customer (which is not unusual, particularly if the customer is a well-known organization assumed to have 'deep pockets'). Well-advised customers may also seek indemnities from vendors with respect to observing the customer's confidentiality requirements, compliance with data protection and other regulatory requirements. Depending on the circumstances, there may also be other important vendor obligations, which should have the backing of an indemnity. It is important that these devices are used carefully, and with advice, so that they are legally effective, and to avoid any inference that they are subject to any of the other exclusions and limitations in the contract.

3. Employment: TUPE

The issues highlighted so far relate very much to the outsourcing services themselves, but the key legal issues associated with outsourcing also include 'people' issues. European outsourcing customers and vendors need to consider and deal with the application of the Transfer of Undertakings (Protection of Employment) Regulations 2006 (TUPE) in the UK, and the local enactment of the Acquired Rights Directive (Directive 2001/23/EC) in certain other European jurisdictions.

The essence of TUPE, in the outsourcing context, is the legal transfer of employees where there is a 'service provision change'. Determining whether TUPE applies in the case of a particular outsourcing is highly technical, but it is often the case that a relevant transfer can occur, where service changes such as the following are made:

- Services are outsourced from a customer to a vendor for the first time as a 'first-generation' outsourcing – for example where a customer, who had previously provided all IT support in-house, contracts with a vendor for the provision of those services.
- Outsourced services are transferred from one vendor to another vendor, usually when a first-generation outsourcing contract has come to an end, and the customer has selected a different vendor (known as 'second-generation outsourcing').

- Where a customer brings the provision of outsourced services back in-house.

Where staff 'TUPE' transfer across to another employer, this happens as a matter of mandatory law (unless the employee objects), which means that the parties cannot exclude its application by including provisions in their contract. Also, the transfer takes place on the same employment terms and conditions that previously applied to the employee, and it will be difficult for the new employer to justify any change where the effect would be to remove or reduce any significant benefit. As the transferee becomes responsible for all costs relating to the transferring employees, this can be the subject of protracted discussions.

Dealing with TUPE is critical in the planning of outsourcing. As well as managing the practical side (such as observing the legally required consultation process, which is often done by the customer's HR team in a first-generation outsourcing), it is usual to include terms in the services contract (or in a specific asset and employee transfer contract), which set out how the parties have agreed to deal with the application of TUPE between themselves. Note that although the parties cannot exclude the application of the legislation, much can be done to manage its effect. In the case of a first-generation outsourcing, the vendor will want the contract to contain warranties from the customer as to existing terms of employment, and that the required information has been given to employees. The parties should agree the apportionment of pay, benefits and responsibility for any claims and, as a way of reinforcing this, they often include indemnities in respect of the period before transfer (given by the customer) and after transfer (given by the vendor). It is also advisable to deal with the potential application of TUPE on termination or expiry of the outsourcing contract because, as noted above, both second-generation outsourcing and bringing outsourced services back in-house can constitute 'service provision changes'.

Conclusion and approach

The three key legal issues detailed above are very likely to arise in some form in most outsourcing transactions, and customers should, from the very early stages of making the decision to outsource and taking steps to select a vendor, be thinking about service scope and standards, as well as risk and TUPE issues. It is important that this focus is maintained and managed throughout the process of drawing up the contractual network that establishes an outsourcing arrangement, so that this network will in turn provide a solid basis for a successful business 'partnership' with the outsourced services vendor.

INSOURCING

The factors that provided a solid case for outsourcing an operation at a given time may become less valid over time. More enlightened companies review these areas periodically, and sometimes find that after a number of years a case can be made for bringing one or more of them back in-house again, ie 'insourcing'. An interesting recent example is Sainsbury's supermarkets. In its 2006–07 annual report, the company revealed: 'We increased our cost savings target to £440 million (from £400 million) following our insourcing of IT in April 2006, and we are on track to deliver this.'

Few companies these days consider insourcing operations that they have never managed internally, but a review of spend areas might suggest some that would be worth reviewing.

7

Negotiation

I'll make him an offer he can't refuse.

(Mario Puzo: The Godfather, *1969)*

This chapter contains:

- The distinction between buying and negotiation.
- Aligning style and tactics with the nature of the buyer–vendor relationship.
- Why most people are poor negotiators.
- How to develop your negotiating abilities.
- The five golden rules of effective negotiation.
- Minimum and maximum settling points (MSPs), and the 'killer question'.
- The buyer's power over the course of the buying cycle.
- How to leverage your buying power.
- Vendor pre-conditioning.

THE DISTINCTION BETWEEN BUYING AND NEGOTIATING

Many people unfamiliar with professional buying practices assume that a buyer would spend most of his working life negotiating. And when asked for the main objective of negotiation, they will usually say it's to reduce costs.

Now here's a conundrum. A search on Amazon's website for books on 'negotiation' brings up 4,508 titles, while 'cost reduction' brings up only 55 – that's 82 titles on the former subject for every one on the latter.

Why are there so many books on negotiation (a tool), and so few on cost reduction (the objective)? I believe it's because there's an exaggerated view of the importance of the role of negotiation in cost reduction, partly because, for many people, negotiation is their sole 'tool in the box' to reduce costs. Negotiation is undoubtedly a fascinating subject in its own right, for intellectual and emotional reasons – what could be more interesting than the challenge of moving the position of the person you're negotiating with nearer to the position you want? But this begs the question of whether you're negotiating with the right vendors, about the right things, at the right time.

The reality is that many successful buyers spend little of their time negotiating with vendors. They spend far more time addressing all the other issues that lead to cost reductions – the very issues that are covered in the other nine chapters of this book.

ALIGNING STYLE AND TACTICS WITH THE NATURE OF THE BUYER–VENDOR RELATIONSHIP

When planning for negotiations, you need to be clear about the type of relationship you are seeking with a vendor in the particular spend area. The spend area's position within the buying portfolio (Chapter 2) will give you a guide. In terms of cost reduction, we are most interested in the 'leverage' and 'strategic' quadrants. Style and tactics are important issues, because they need to be modified to suit the different quadrants.

Buying in the leverage quadrant

In this quadrant, you are a significant buyer in the marketplace – vendors are probably beating a path to your door – but you do not need a harmonious, long-term relationship with vendors. You are the more powerful party in the relationship. There are many vendors, and dropping existing vendors and adopting new ones is reasonably problem-free, so your prime challenge is simply to obtain the required quality of goods or services, at the lowest cost you can achieve. This will inevitably make the incumbent vendor's salesperson unhappy, which may make you uncomfortable. But, as we shall see shortly, the first golden rule of negotiating is 'Accept you are paid to feel uncomfortable'.

Buying in the strategic quadrant

In this quadrant, you may or may not be a significant buyer in the marketplace, but you need to foster good relationships over a long period, with one or two vendors. You need a continuous and harmonious relationship, and will probably be engaged in joint problem solving. You will need good interpersonal skills to work with both the vendor and internal stakeholders over the long term.

WHY MOST PEOPLE ARE POOR NEGOTIATORS

Most people are poor negotiators, but this should not be surprising. How often in modern life are we called upon to negotiate? Almost everything we buy has a fixed 'price tag', and we therefore have very little chance to practise. But I think we have to consider cause and effect here. Perhaps most items have fixed price tags because people feel really uncomfortable when they have to negotiate?

Among other activities, my company runs negotiation workshops. During these workshops, many delegates are happy to admit that they find the whole process of negotiating uncomfortable, sometimes to a debilitating degree. It surprises some people when they hear that almost everyone else is similarly afflicted. In understanding this common issue, we can begin to consider how to turn it into a significant advantage. More on this later.

HOW TO IMPROVE YOUR NEGOTIATING ABILITIES

The individual who likes to learn through reading specialist books is spoilt for choice when it comes to negotiation. But there's a problem, and that's the matter of 'negotiation philosophy'. Two of the three current bestselling negotiation book titles on the Amazon website should illustrate the point: *Negotiation – Harvard Business Essentials –* '...drawing on rich content from Harvard Business School Publishing';

Bare Knuckle Negotiating – '...knockout negotiation tactics they won't teach you at Business School'. The key point is that different negotiating styles and tactics are suitable for different scenarios.

Given the likely return on investment from negotiation courses, I would also recommend that you attend courses run by independent companies and professional bodies. CIPS has long run a number of courses, for all levels of experience and expertise.

THE FIVE GOLDEN RULES OF EFFECTIVE NEGOTIATION

It is beyond the scope of this chapter to convert you into an effective negotiator. However, I can share some of the key factors that you will need to consider if you are to improve your performance. This learning is based on many years of experience in conducting negotiations, for many goods and services, in many sectors.

First, you should forget about achieving 'an amicable compromise that benefits all parties' or 'win/win' outcomes. For those of us who ply our trade in the more commercial aspects of society, I suggest an alternative definition of a successful negotiation – 'getting exactly what you want, and leaving nothing on the table'.

These rules are best applied during the negotiation meeting, after you have decided you wish to appoint the vendor in question, but also wish to improve further on the terms of the vendor's offer, most probably in the area of price. Having managed the buying cycle proficiently, you will be in the happy position of having other viable vendors with which you may continue discussions, should the meeting not result in the outcome you're seeking.

The five golden rules will help you begin to improve your negotiating ability. If you find them obvious, my challenge is that the overwhelming majority of people don't act in this way, and I doubt that you do.

1. Accept that you are paid to feel uncomfortable

Most people find the process of negotiation uncomfortable. Of course, the extent of discomfort varies significantly between individuals, but few people can claim total immunity. One major difficulty with negotiation is that we have to control our actions, as well as those of our opponents. In other words, we have to control and manipulate a situation involving others, who often have conflicting interests to our own. My experience is that most people find it difficult to control themselves in negotiation situations, let alone the other party.

I don't really have a simple solution for avoiding this discomfort, other than to suggest you realize that everyone feels it to some extent, and you tell yourself that (at least in commercial situations) you are paid to feel uncomfortable. Of course, realizing that our opponents may be feeling anxious or stressed provides an opportunity to take advantage of the phenomenon. Many people just want the negotiation to end, so if someone suggests that you 'split the difference' or 'meet halfway', take it as a sign that they wish the process to end. Hold on, and don't concede. You will usually get 100 per cent of the value under discussion.

You may be thinking that I am suggesting a negotiation style that is hard, aggressive – even rude. Nothing could be further from the truth. The best negotiators I have seen are polite, and appear to be fair and reasonable, yet underneath have a steely determination to maximize results for their organization. Being firm is not the same as being rude, and being a tough negotiator is in no way related to being nasty.

In a similar vein, I have witnessed excellent negotiators who adopt a variety of personal styles. If you are a mild-mannered, reflective, analytical kind of person, you can be a very effective negotiator; you just need to ensure that your style provides enough evidence of your assertiveness. At the other end of the spectrum, if you are a larger than life, dynamic and outwardly energetic person, you too can achieve fantastic results; just don't let your ego and exuberance get in the way. Self-awareness tends to be a trait of effective negotiators, so reflect on your own style, and its associated strengths and limitations.

2. The market does not rule

Economists tell us that the price of something is set by the supply and demand curves pertaining to the good or service in question. This may well be correct, but as a usable commercial tool it is worthless. It provides no indication of how much we should pay for electricity, baked beans, or anything else for that matter. Of course, economists are correct in highlighting that the price of something is related to what one person will sell for, and what another person will pay, but in the commercial world we are dealing with real individuals, not aggregated supply and demand patterns. When individuals are presented with the same information, they interpret their own requirements differently, and will accept a very broad range of outcomes. Give 10 people the same car to buy, and you can expect 10 different prices. For most goods and services, the market does not rule, and you must negotiate effectively with each individual that you are presented with.

3. It's about them, not you

In negotiations, people focus on their own problems and requirements:

- 'We can't afford to lose this contract.'
- 'I have to win this work.'
- 'I must have this car.'

The effect of such self-focus can be summarized in the phrase 'If you want it badly, you'll get it badly'. In any negotiation, focus on the other party. What are they looking to achieve? What are their circumstances? What other options do they have? What is their level of urgency?

Finding the answers to these questions can transform your relative bargaining power, and also ensures that you avoid dwelling on your own difficulties.

4. The more you ask for, the more you get. The less you ask for, the less you get

The truth of this statement is based on both experience and empirical evidence. Having analysed data from 28 workshops, each comprising four sets of six negotiations, the highest opening price achieved the highest finally agreed price on 87 per cent of occasions. Conversely, the lowest opening price resulted in the lowest finally agreed price on 82 per cent of occasions. There is a powerful correlation between your starting point and end point.

If your expectations are low, your results will be low. Do not be fair and reasonable. Be greedy.

5. Think in small numbers

In negotiations people often move around in large, round numbers. I have experienced negotiations in corporate life where people move their bids around in sizeable 'chunks', often £10,000, £20,000 etc. People also tend to think in terms of round percentages – often 5 or 10 per cent. Large amounts of money are given away by thinking in round numbers.

Ask for much, and if pushed to concede, do so in small quantities, slowly. If you do nothing else, this will significantly improve your performance.

MINIMUM AND MAXIMUM SETTLING POINTS (MSPS), AND THE 'KILLER QUESTION'

Both buyers and vendors should set MSPs: for the buyer, the MSP is the maximum settling point, ie the price above which they will not pay for the good or service; for the vendor, the MSP is the minimum settling point, ie the price below which they will not sell their good or service. The vendor doesn't have to be happy to sell at the MSP – merely prepared to do so.

The challenge for both parties is to drive the other party to their MSP. The buyer needs to ask open questions, aimed at testing the willingness of the vendor to reduce their price. There could be many reasons why the vendor would be prepared to do this, including:

- a wish to gain (or at least not lose) market share;
- a wish to avoid a cash-flow crisis;
- a wish on the part of the salesman to land this order and win a larger commission or bonus – never underestimate a salesman's willingness to put his own interests before those of his company;
- the buyer may buy second-hand equipment in the marketplace;
- a new model is going to be released shortly, which will reduce the sellability (and therefore the obtainable price) of the current model.

And so on. By the negotiating stage of the buying cycle, assuming the process has been competently executed, you will be in a powerful negotiating position:

- You have a shortlist of viable vendors, actively competing for your business.
- In cases where you have formally outlined the possibility of the lowest initial bid being accepted, and assuming no collusion among the vendors, the vendors should have made an offering not far above their MSP. If this is the case, there may not be a large gap between your MSP and their MSP to bridge at the meeting.
- Vendors will already have invested significant effort in their bids, and won't want to see that effort wasted (as would be the case if they don't emerge from the process with a contract).

However, a note of warning. For even experienced buyers, there may be a significant gap between where the potential vendors' MSPs lie, and their pricing position at the start of the negotiation process. The next case study provides an example.

CASE STUDY: WHAT SHOULD YOU DO WITH AN OFFER YOU CAN'T REFUSE? REFUSE IT!

We need to recognize that potential vendors sometimes have a joint interest in maintaining a buyer's illusions in some areas, and I came across a good example some years ago.

I was working for a client and seeking to negotiate a multi-million-pound print management contract – the successful bidder would get all of my client's print business for a period of four years. My client's print manager was extremely experienced, and an enthusiastic exponent of regular market testing. His 'expert' view was that we would secure only a small cost reduction (2–4 per cent) through a single vendor contract, but that there were a range of 'soft' reasons to justify negotiating such a contract.

Now the UK print market is fiercely competitive, partly due to the extent to which e-auctions are used to buy print (see Chapter 9 for information on e-auctions). We quickly reached a shortlist of three major potential vendors, and each put forward proposals that would have given my client small cost reductions, in line with the print manager's expectations. Lengthy negotiations with all three companies failed to result in any clear leader in pricing terms. We were becoming persuaded that we had reached something close to the vendor's MSPs.

Then the unexpected happened. The chief executive of one of the three vendors decided that he was going to make 'an offer that we couldn't refuse', contractually guaranteeing minimum savings of 10 per cent. Experience has taught me to proceed cautiously with unexpectedly attractive commercial offers, so I told him we'd reflect on it, and possibly give the other bidders a chance to look again at *their* bids.

And so began the process so loved by buyers, and so hated by vendors, the 'Dutch auction'. Both the alternative vendors made attractive counter-offers within 24 hours, and the next two weeks were spent receiving a succession of increasingly attractive counter-offers. The final cost reduction was 29 per cent, and the contract was awarded to the company which had first made 'the offer we couldn't refuse'.

Now let's say the negotiation has arrived at the point that the vendor is simply unwilling to improve their offer. It's time to consider asking the 'killer question'.

'If that's really your final offer, you wouldn't be upset by my awarding the business to another viable vendor, if their bid were £1,000 lower than yours?'

I've very rarely had the response 'no' to the killer question. Salesmen will often challenge the implicit view that their company's offering isn't superior to their competitors' offerings, so the bids could not be comparable. After listening politely to such waffle, ask the salesman for the price point at which he would not be upset by the business being awarded elsewhere. The answer may surprise you.

Salesmen will usually be limited as to how far they can drop a price without authorization from their boss. So it's usually a good sign when the salesman asks for 'time out' to call his boss, in an effort to secure the low price you're seeking – but recognize that this might also be a tactical ploy, and people who've bought double-glazed windows for their homes may have come across it. The following case study is about this ploy.

CASE STUDY: WHEN I'M BUYING WINDOWS

Some years ago, I decided to order replacement double-glazed windows for my home. One vendor's salesman was trying every trick in the book to persuade me to commit to a deal there and then. He'd started at £20,000 but, after some time, he'd dropped the price to £12,000. I said I simply couldn't afford a penny over £8,000, and I stuck doggedly to that position. He then appeared to become agitated at my continuing resistance to agreeing a deal at £12,000, and the atmosphere became very frosty for a time. Then a thought occurred to him, apparently out of the blue. On the pretext that he couldn't drop the price any further without the authorization of his sales director, he called him from his mobile phone. The conversation went along the following lines:

Hello John, I'm sorry, I know you're on honeymoon in Barbados, but I'm really keen to see what we can do to get down to Mr Buchanan's target price of £8,000. What's that John? You're not best pleased at being disturbed on holiday? I'm really sorry, but I'll buy you a case of champagne if we land this order. I started with our list price, £20,000 for 14 windows, a total area of 100 square metres. But Mr Buchanan is a very tough negotiator, and he's driven me to the highest discount level I'm allowed to offer, 40 per cent, so a price of £12,000. What's that John? £8,000 is far lower than we could ever go, given the quality of our windows, which are far superior to our competitors' windows, and £12,000 is a rock-bottom price? But Mr Buchanan simply can't afford that. What's that John? You're prepared for me to go as low as £11,000 if Mr Buchanan commits tonight, and even then only because you're in a great mood, watching a beautiful sunset? Wow, thanks John, I'll put that to Mr Buchanan…

Now – clearly not realized by the salesman – his mobile phone was one of those where it was all too easy to hear what the other person was saying, and the purported 'sales director' was a woman. Nothing unusual in that, of course, but I did enjoy her closing remark, 'Good luck, darling, when do you think you'll be home for dinner?'

I refused the £11,000 offer, and an extremely disgruntled salesman left my house, after a long evening. I decided to leave the matter there for a few weeks, judging that the company would get increasingly concerned that I might place the business with another company. Just a few days later, I received a call from the company, asking whether I wanted to go ahead with an order for £11,000. I explained that my best offer was still £8,000 and told them I was to meet with another manufacturer the next day, in order to 'focus their minds' and try to bring the matter to a close.

Ten minutes later, I had another call from the company, quite cheerfully accepting my offer of £8,000. The windows were excellent, and were fitted speedily and expertly. The window quality would not have been any better, nor would they have been fitted any more speedily or expertly, had I paid the £11,000 sought by the salesman. But I hazard a guess that he'd have been very happy to win an extra £3,000 commission for one evening's work.

THE BUYER'S POWER OVER THE COURSE OF THE BUYING CYCLE

Your power to drive the vendor from the pricing point he wants to sell for, to the lowest point that he's prepared to sell for, increases over the course of the buying cycle (see Figure 7.1).

Basic human nature is behind this phenomenon. The more time and effort a vendor puts into landing a contract, the more flexible he will be to improve his bid, to levels he would not have countenanced at the outset of the process. So when you have the shortlist of vendors, be sure to make them work hard to improve their bids.

An obvious implication of Figure 7.1 is that the vendor is unlikely to make significant concessions after the buyer has communicated the decision to award him the contract. And yet I've seen buyers trying to renegotiate contracts at this stage, when they've suddenly thought about some issues or – even worse – in response to one of the other potential vendors dropping his price. When another vendor drops their price after the buyer has made a commitment to go elsewhere, it's a sure sign that the vendor hasn't understood – or more likely, pretends they haven't understood – the need to put in their 'final offer' at the appropriate time. For the sake of your reputation, and

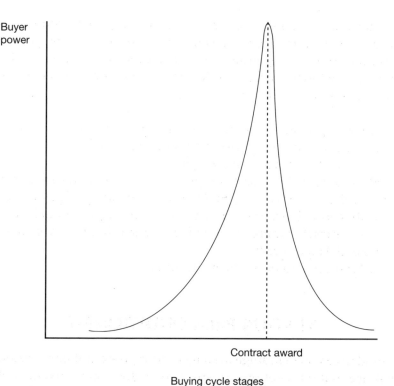

Figure 7.1 *The development of a buyer's power over the course of the buying cycle*

future credibility with vendors, you should always reject offers made after a clearly communicated deadline.

HOW TO LEVERAGE YOUR BUYING POWER

What can you do to make your business more attractive to the marketplace in general and individual vendors in particular? You can't change your company's overall demand for a particular good or service over the short to medium term (other than stockpiling goods or bringing forward service usage), although a reasonable expectation of increasing demand is helpful. But you can effectively increase your leverage through offering longer-term contracts – be sure to allow contractually for the possibility that, post contract award, other vendors may offer either lower prices or attractive innovations. This matter is covered in Chapter 8.

Other than volumes, there are a number of things you can do to become a more attractive customer, to leverage your buying power and secure more favourable terms. They include the following; some of them might be included within tender documentation, others conveyed during face-to-face meetings:

- Offer to give the vendor a testimonial (verbal or written) if the contract works out well – buyers tend to trust other buyers, particularly those working in the same sector.
- Stress the prestige aspect of supplying your company (if there is one).
- Give the impression that you'll be pleasant and professional to deal with, and will ensure your company's managers' compliance with the contract (where the vendor might otherwise see this as a potential area of risk).
- Offer speedy invoice settlement terms.

VENDOR PRE-CONDITIONING

I would urge you to indulge in some vendor pre-conditioning before the final negotiation meeting. Irrespective of the competitiveness of the vendor's bid, tell them well in advance of the meeting that they're not competitive. There are at least four reasons for this:

- The vendor's bid is based on their own circumstances, and the fact that their bid is currently the most competitive is quite irrelevant. They may well be willing to concede further ground, but could scarcely be expected to do so, should they learn it's the best offer you have available.
- The vendor will have time to explore with colleagues just how far the bid can be improved.
- The vendor will be grateful to you that despite being uncompetitive, you're still willing to spend your time with them, in an effort to give them a better chance of being awarded the contract.
- Other vendors may improve their bids during further meetings with them.

I rarely tell vendors who the other vendors are, a viable tactic if there are a large number of potential vendors. Why would I encourage collusion? And I never give details of other vendors' bids, or tell them how far they need to improve their bid. Salesmen have a multitude of ways of getting insights into other vendors' bids, often by saying something along the lines of 'OK, what do we need to do on pricing to win this contract – are we talking 5 per cent? 10 per cent?'. Tell them you're not willing to divulge this information, for the simple reason that it would be breaking commercial confidentiality. They can hardly argue with this, as they reasonably expect confidentiality with respect to their own submissions.

8

Contracts and contract law

All sensible people are selfish, and nature is tugging at every contract to make the
terms of it fair.

(Ralph Waldo Emerson: The conduct of life, *1860)*

This chapter contains:

- Why formal contracts are important.
- Contract fairness.
- Contract duration.
- Which contract terms to use.
- Vendor terms to be challenged.
- Developing your own contract terms.
- Contract termination.
- Contract terms and the buying cycle.
- Contract register.

You can speedily learn much about contracts and contract law from
specialist courses and books, but for obvious reasons they cannot place
the subject within the particular commercial scenarios you are facing,
which raises questions such as:

- What contract duration would be appropriate for this good / service?
- Which contract terms should I use – those sourced from a third party, or my own company's terms, or the vendor's terms, new terms altogether, or some combination of all these?
- What issues might lead me to want to terminate a contract in this area, and what contract terms would enable me to terminate the contract?
- There's a lot of uncertainty about my company's future demand for this good or service – how might the contract best reflect this?

The objective of this chapter is to provide you with guidance for answering such questions.

WHY FORMAL CONTRACTS ARE IMPORTANT

Many executives find contracts, and contract law, both difficult to understand and boring – an unfortunate combination. They are also often envious of the remuneration of lawyers, and this sometimes leads them to avoid negotiating formal contracts, whenever and wherever they can. They typically make an agreement on the basis that 'their word is their bond', and some important details of the commitment are 'agreed' verbally, but not put into writing.

I've had to resolve many problems arising from executives' aversion to formal contracts. On the other hand, I've had to pay little attention to properly constructed formal contracts. Even where they are disadvantageous to my client, they can often be renegotiated, or in the worst-case scenario will run their course, allowing a new contract to be negotiated – possibly with a new vendor.

It's my experience that most senior executives are well capable of understanding the 99 per cent of contract terms that do not merit expert legal opinion or explanation. Confusion may sometimes arise from a vendor's use of opaque legal terminology. In such cases, tell the vendor to translate the term(s) into plain English, or you won't contract with them. Unless they're a monopoly vendor, or a near-monopoly vendor, they'll almost certainly do as you ask. This may leave a small number of terms that are simply difficult to understand. In that case, you should seek expert legal advice.

CONTRACT FAIRNESS

Let me make something clear immediately. If you are serious about wanting to reduce your company's costs, and you are not pursuing 'softer agendas' such as outlined in Appendix 4, you need to clear your mind of the concept of 'fairness'. It will add nothing to your thinking processes, and will sow the seeds of confusion. It is your job to obtain goods and services on the most commercially advantageous terms you can. That's a challenging objective in itself, so why saddle yourself with others?

CONTRACT DURATION

I am often struck by the high proportion of contracts which are one year long, or multiples thereof. Why not 9 months? 21 months? Optimal contract duration results from a number of considerations, including the following.

1. The anticipated resources required to market test

The resources you need to commit in order to market test a spend area may be substantial on the first occasion. But, having made insights into the marketplace on the first occasion, the resources required will be less when you market test again.

Resources are always limited, so if you spend a great deal of time on market-testing one area, other areas are likely to be neglected. Broadly speaking, the longer the period required to market test an area, the longer the contract should be. But longer contracts need special attention to the circumstances under which they may be terminated, for example in the case of general marketplace price falls, which would otherwise make the contract commercially disadvantageous to the buyer.

Adjust individual contract durations so as to spread contract expiry dates throughout the year, in order to more evenly spread your workload. I'll pick up on this point again at the end of this chapter, in the context of contract registers.

2. The anticipated resources required to take on, and manage, new vendors in the spend area

Depending on the spend area, the resources may be anywhere in a continuum from negligible to considerable. Clearly, contract duration needs to reflect this reality. So if the resources are negligible, consider a short contract, perhaps up to a year's duration. If sizeable, go for a longer contract – possibly two or three years' duration.

3. The number of viable vendors

A buyer always likes to have a large number of viable vendors, but for a variety of reasons, vendor numbers are small in some sectors, and one vendor may even enjoy a monopoly. All else being equal, the smaller the number of viable vendors, the longer should be the contract.

4. The incidence of innovation in the marketplace

Marketplaces vary greatly in the extent to which innovations arrive over time. For example, in the case of consumer electronic goods – televisions, say – innovations come along at a blistering rate, from a number of manufacturers. If you were a buyer for an independent electronics retailer, you clearly wouldn't want to tie yourself contractually to just one manufacturer.

All else being equal, the greater the likelihood and frequency of innovation in a particular marketplace, the shorter should be the contract durations, and the greater your exposure to many vendors.

5. The anticipated importance of personal relationships in the success (or failure) of a contract in this area

In many spend areas there is little need for successful personal relationships. I'd like to think that if you were to order your stationery from vendor x under a contract, the correct goods will turn up on time, at the right place, and the right price will be invoiced in due course. You really don't need to have a personal relationship with the salesman.

But some spend areas are different, and it could be that it's important for you – or one or more of your colleagues – to have a good working relationship with key executive(s) in the vendor. Your company may rely on their creativity, knowledge of highly technical matters, or other issues.

However, a problem sometimes emerges, and I've seen it most often in the area of buying marketing services (creative input, design, strategic planning etc). A marketing executive will regard a certain individual or company as critical to the success of a project: 'We simply MUST have Eleanor Mannington-Withers do this work – nobody else is in her league!' So a contract is negotiated, during the course of which your colleague leaves your company. His replacement hasn't even heard of Eleanor Mannington-Withers, and seeks to cancel the contract in favour of a new one with Bill Smith – 'Nobody else is in his league!'

One obvious solution to this problem is to have a contract term that allows for termination in x weeks, for any reason deemed adequate by the buyer.

6. The volatility of pricing in the marketplace over time

Marketplace pricing volatility may arise from a number of sources, but the most common are:

- steady falls in product price/utility ratios over time – eg electronic goods, white goods;
- impact of major raw material price fluctuations – eg the impact of oil price movements on the price of motor fuels;
- impact of exchange rate movements on the cost of imported goods.

The challenge in such markets is to have clear contract terms under which the contract may be terminated, and possibly also contract terms to reflect changes in the vendor's raw material costs, or movements in relevant exchange rates. The topics of raw material costs and exchange rate movements are covered in Chapter 4.

7. The potential benefits flowing from longer-term contracts

Most buyers would agree that there need to be good reasons to enter into longer-term agreements, as they remove the buyer's company from engagement with the wider marketplace for the contract duration. In his book on negotiating commercial contracts (Sheridan, 1991), the author convincingly outlines his view that the justification for entering into long-term contracts needs to be founded on an analysis of each individual requirement, rather than applying an all-embracing philosophy. The following questions would need to be answered:

- Is there a price benefit that can be sustained throughout the contract's life, which would not otherwise be likely to occur by more regular reviews?
- Is the supply side of the market for that particular product already 'controlled' by, say, only three or four major vendors?

- Will the contract include a guarantee that the vendor's production line, or an agreed part of it, will be dedicated to the buyer's demands?
- Will the deal provide the certainty of access to new technology, whether introduced by the selected vendor or his competitors?
- Are there to be proper provisions for market collapse – ie a major revision in the buying habits of consumers, on which the buyer's company is ultimately dependent for sales?
- If any long-term contract is to be coupled with a major reduction in the number of vendors used by the buyer, are the intended contracted vendors capable of carrying the burden of, say, sole or dual supply in respect of a vital item?
- In the event of non-supply under the terms of the contract, whether due to _force majeure_ or mismanagement by the vendors, what provisions are available to the buyer to obtain continuity of supply elsewhere?

But even if all the above issues are adequately considered, there remains the possibility that your business requirements may change to the extent that you need – or wish – to terminate the contract early, and possibly well before its scheduled termination date. The various reasons may not be reasonably predictable at the point of contract commitment, but the problem needs to be recognized all the same. You should therefore have a clause in the contract that permits you to 'buy your way out', and terminate it early. Again, you need to use competition to your advantage, so include a term within your proposed contract to handle the issue. Under normal circumstances, the sum required to 'buy your way out' should decline over the contract period, possibly falling to zero in the final year of two.

WHICH CONTRACT TERMS TO USE

Given the point that 'fairness' is not a helpful concept in the area of contract terms, the preference should always be to contract on your company's contract terms wherever possible, suitably modified to reflect the spend area in question. Those terms should not seek to be 'fair' – they should protect your company's interests. But this will not always be possible, especially when the vendor is in a powerful enough position to insist that their contract terms be used. It is rare, however, to find a vendor who will not agree to change any of their contract terms, especially when they believe you may have viable alternative vendors. I have negotiated many contracts where only a few of the vendor's standard terms were particularly objectionable and had to be omitted or modified, eg a right for the vendor to increase prices without the buyer having a consequent right to terminate the contract.

Ensure that a term is included to the effect that the contract is made under the jurisdiction of your own country's legal system, something along the following lines:

> Governing law and jurisdiction: This Agreement, and any dispute or claim arising out of, or in connection with, it or its subject matter, shall be governed by, and construed in accordance with, the law of England and Wales. The parties irrevocably agree that the courts of England and Wales shall have exclusive jurisdiction to settle any dispute or claim that arises out of, or in connection with, this Agreement, or its subject matter.

VENDOR TERMS TO BE CHALLENGED

A number of terms frequently appear within vendors' own contract terms, which need to be challenged and omitted. I find the following two appearing regularly, but I've yet to come across a vendor who is unwilling to remove them upon request.

1. Automatic contract extensions

Many vendors' contract terms include something of this nature. Usually, the buyer is required to send a written termination notice to the vendor some time before the end of the contract, often months before – or the contract will automatically be extended for a period of a year, sometimes longer.

2. Vendor's right to adjust selling prices

Where I find an 'automatic contract extension' clause in a vendor's terms, I expect to find a term of this nature also. Basically, it allows the vendor to raise prices without reference to the buyer, and the buyer will be obliged to pay the higher prices. Sometimes the contract term will allude to the need to increase prices to reflect higher costs of labour, utilities etc.

DEVELOPING YOUR OWN CONTRACT TERMS

If you're in the position of not having any 'company standard terms' for the buying of goods and/or services, how might you go about developing them? Any commercial lawyer will be able to supply you with standard terms, otherwise you might buy standard terms off one of a number of companies that supply through the internet – search 'standard contract terms' and a number will come up. But do recognize that material quality will be variable if you take the latter approach.

From time to time you will come across situations where standard terms are simply not up to the task, or you feel there are some potential serious risks in the contract. I would generally recommend the use of a good commercial lawyer at this point. Now many people are put off this course of action because of the cost, but if you plan carefully for the meeting, it's amazing how much advice and guidance you can gather in an hour or two. And the cost will probably be trivial compared with the costs you'll incur if matters go awry in the absence of legal advice.

CONTRACT TERMINATION

There are many circumstances under which you might wish to end a contract before its natural expiry date, and your contract terms need to cover them. The more important ones are the following.

1. Vendor's failure to meet contractual requirements

There are numerous ways in which vendors may fail to meet contractual requirements. Depending on the specific reason(s) in a particular case, you may judge that it is worth pressing the vendor to meet their contractual obligations, or invoking your legal options. In many cases, however – and particularly when the personal relationships have become difficult – you may simply decide that you wish to replace the vendor.

It is important that you specify in the contract exactly what is required from the vendors in terms of specification, delivery timeliness, and poooibly much more besides. And contract terms need to make very clear the circumstances in which you will have the right to terminate the contract early, and how many days' notice you have to give the vendor – a right which you may (or may not) choose to exercise in individual cases.

There is an inherent conflict in just how difficult contractual requirements are made. If they are made very tight – 'stretch targets' as they're sometimes called – it's likely that the vendor will repeatedly fail, and become dispirited, with little benefit to either party. On the other hand, if the requirements are too easy to deliver, the vendor will not be driven to make significant efforts.

Non-buyers often try to introduce penalties – financial or otherwise – into contracts, in an effort to 'force' vendors to honour their commitments. But under the laws of England and Wales, such penalty clauses would not be enforceable. The best approach is to negotiate a contract term for 'liquidated damages', whereby the parties agree a genuine pre-estimate of the financial damage that would face the buyer in the event of, say, late delivery of goods. And it's important to understand that there's no point in cloaking a penalty clause under the term 'liquidated damages', as it would remain unenforceable.

2. Loss of vendors' key staff

In some contracts, one or more of a number of the vendor's directors or employees may be deemed critical to the performance of the contract, whether by virtue of their expertise, experience, or other matters. So their absence if they left the company – or partial absence, eg if their time devoted to your contract were reduced – would have a damaging impact on your business, and you would then wish to have an option to terminate the contract.

I recently negotiated a contract for a client where the continuation of three directors at the vendor was deemed so critical that the following term was employed:

> KEY EMPLOYEES
> The Buyer considers the retention by the Seller, of the services of all three Key Employees on a full-time working basis, to be critical to the successful working of the Agreement. Should any of the Key Employees cease to work full-time for the Seller during the term of the Agreement, the Buyer will have the option to terminate the Agreement, after 12 weeks' written notice.

3. Major differences in actual demand from forecast demand, whether in terms of volumes or specifications

If 'the only constant is change', as the saying goes, we have to expect actual demand to differ from forecast demand – certainly in terms of volumes, but also (in some cases) in terms of specifications.

Vendors become understandably frustrated by buyers who habitually negotiate contracts with especially favourable terms for high forecast demands, and – if and when actual demand is far lower than forecast demand – the buyer is unsympathetic to vendor pleas for more realistic prices.

But there's a good way to address this issue, and that is to negotiate retrospective payments, ie payments from the seller to the buyer, in recognition of actual demand exceeding a certain level of demand (say, 50 per cent of forecast demand). The payment is normally paid after each 12 months' trading period, but of course there's no reason why the period should not be longer or shorter. The period of 12 months is often taken because it ties in with the accounting reporting periods of companies, and most executives tend to think in terms of annual sales.

An alternative approach would be to introduce a contract term stating that the buyer does not guarantee to order any minimum quantity of goods or services from the vendor. In the event of any dissatisfaction with the contract, of a nature which would not otherwise give the buyer a right to terminate the contract, this term could be invoked, and the buyer can then start ordering from other vendors.

4. Marketplace changes which lead to the contract becoming commercially disadvantageous to the buyer

Another marketplace change the buyer has to guard against, especially in a contract over a period of several years, is that the price in the contract becomes uncompetitive over time, for any one of a number of reasons. On a number of occasions, to guard against this very possibility, I've used a clause drawn from Sheridan's 1991 book:

> Competitive activity: if at any time during the contract period two other substantially sized, competent and established suppliers in the same line of business as the Sellers, each simultaneously offers to deliver goods of acceptable specification, and each in volumes not greater than the annual quantity next to be supplied under the terms of this contract, at prices more than (say) 0,5% below the prices then in force under the terms of this contract (before the deduction of 'contract' discount as hereinafter described), then the Sellers will, within four weeks, reduce their then-current price(s), to a level which will produce prices, before the deduction of 'contract' discount, equal to the average of the competitive offers.

Any such prices thus arrived at, will form the new basis for any future price variations. The Sellers have the right to ask the Buyers to produce written evidence of any such competitive price offers. In the event that matching the average of the two competitors' offers would necessitate a reduction in the Sellers' current price(s) of more than, (say) 5%, the Sellers may decline to match this competition, by giving four weeks' written notice to the Buyers, after which the contract may be terminated without penalty to either party.

Consideration also needs to be given to the possibility that another vendor comes up with an innovation of which you would wish to take advantage, but are unable to do so because of your existing contract. Now you would not normally wish to negotiate long-term contracts in markets where innovations are frequent, but from time to time even the most 'basic' market will generate innovations. The answer is to have a contract clause that gives you the right to terminate the contract early, in the event of you wishing to take advantage of marketplace innovations.

5. Personality clashes

In an ideal world, personality clashes wouldn't happen. But even among experienced buyers, who usually deal with many companies and many more executives in the course of a year, personality clashes are not unknown – although in my personal experience, such clashes are sometimes alleged by vendors who (understandably) aren't happy with my efforts to reduce their prices, and through this tactic, they seek to gain a more sympathetic audience with my client's senior executives.

If genuine personality clashes with buyers are rare, they're perhaps less rare with other executives – which can be unfortunate if one of your senior colleagues has a personality clash with a senior executive at one of your vendors. In my experience, such clashes tend to come about where the vendor offers some sort of creative service, or anything which by its nature is ill-defined. Consultancy services sometimes come into this category, particularly where the scope of the assignment is ill-defined by its very nature.

One approach is to have a contract term to the effect that your company may unilaterally terminate the contract with x weeks' notice, without having to give a reason.

CONTRACT TERMS AND THE BUYING CYCLE

Assuming you're going to use your own contract terms, what is the best time to show them to the potential vendors? In my view, the best time is when the vendor is most amenable, and in this context that means you should include your terms with the tender document, whether it be a request for quotation, or one of the alternatives outlined in Chapter 5. The reason is simple. The vendor will know they're one of a number of potential vendors, and they may already have invested some time and effort into the process, eg helped you develop specifications or a service level agreement. Now the tender document should include something in the nature of the following text, extracted from the RFP template in Appendix 2:

> Contract terms
> The attached contract terms will apply to this contract. If any terms are unacceptable to you, please outline your reasons, and where appropriate, offer alternative terms. Please be aware that your willingness to comply with our terms will be one of the key criteria in our evaluation of your proposal.

Faced with this, it would be a brave potential vendor who raised objections to your contract terms, because they'll judge – probably correctly – that at least some of the other potential vendors won't raise objections. Raising objections runs the risk of elimination from the whole process, and in my experience, very few vendors object to contract terms when they are introduced in this manner.

CONTRACT REGISTER

Many organizations do not have a formal process for keeping track of their contracts, and it can happen that a vendor fails to inform the buyer of an approaching contract end, or they may only inform the buyer a short time before the contract end. This places the buyer in a weak position, because they will not then have enough time in which to carry out key activities such as market research.

But there's a very simple solution to this problem, and that's a contract register. The register can take a number of forms, but one approach that has worked well for me over many years has been to place details of all supply contracts onto an Excel spreadsheet. A simple example is given in Table 8.1.

Table 8.1 Contract register example

Good/ service	Vendor	Contract start date	Contract duration (months)	Contract expiry date	Deadline for starting a review
Creative services	Blue Sky Thinking (Wakefield) Ltd	80401	12	90331	90101
Polythene granules	Polygran Ltd	80201	18	90731	90501
Corrugated boxes	Packit Ltd	80301	24	100228	100101

Note that the dates in three of the columns are in 'yymmdd' order (to end December 2009), or 'yymmdd' order (from the start of January 2010). Now this is important, because through the use of Excel's functionality you need to sort the table in ascending date order, based on the dates in the final column. In this way, you'll have a ready-made list of priorities.

The contract register is also very useful in another way. It enables you to clearly spot where the expiry dates of a number of contracts are near one another. Armed with this information, you'll be able to set new contract durations, so as to help you even out the contract renegotiation workload. Why have a 12-month-long contract, when a 14-month-long one – or 17 months, or whatever – will help avoid work overload?

9

E-procurement

Through e-auctions, we've saved £3.5m pa (27%) on a £13 million pa spend across 18 areas, in just two months.

(The Boots Company plc)

This chapter contains:

- Background.
- Terminology.
- The development of e-procurement.
- A brief introduction to auctions – Dutch, Chinese, Reverse, Electronic, English....
- E-auction 'do's and don'ts'.
- eWorld.
- An overview of e-procurement – The Aberdeen Group.
- E-procurement enabler 1 – Procuri.
- E-procurement enabler 2 – BravoSolution.
- E-procurement enabler 3 – Vendigital.

BACKGROUND

Let's say you're a significant buyer of a good or service, its specification is unambiguous, and numerous vendors are seeking your custom. Your 'dream tool' might be something that had vendors bidding in real time against one another, over a defined period of time, with them seeing other vendors' competing bids (but not knowing the other vendors' identity, for fear of collusion). Wouldn't that be the ultimate 'commoditizing tool', driving vendors relentlessly to their minimum selling prices, with little effort on your part? Oh, and you might want to do all of this without needing to bother issuing hard-copy documentation.

Well, the 'dream tool' has been used by some major organizations for a number of years now, and it's called the 'e-auction'. It's one element in the 'e-procurement' cycle, although sometimes the only one used by organizations, in particular spend areas. It's steadily changing the face of procurement, for those spend areas where organizations can say 'yes' to the following key questions:

- Can we define a clear specification for the spend area?
- Is there a competitive vendor pool?
- Is the spend or unit volume significant enough to be of interest to vendors?
- Are we prepared to change vendor(s) based upon the auction results?

TERMINOLOGY

What is the difference between procurement and e-procurement? On the face of it, it's quite simple. The prefix 'e-' simply denotes that the latter is electronically enabled. That is, an approach that enables companies to communicate with interested parties via the internet.

But electronic enablement delivers far more than you might imagine. Not only does it enable you to do things differently, it enables you to do different things. Enlightened organizations are using e-procurement to deliver some astonishing cost savings, as well as streamlining processes and delivering numerous other benefits. And it's not just private sector organizations. The UK's National Health Service forecasts over £100 million savings will be realized, following a recent three-day-long e-auction for temporary labour. The case study is provided later in this chapter, along with others.

You may recall the buying cycle from Chapter 3. All the cycle stages that involve communicating with potential vendors may be e-enabled. Whether it makes sense to do so, in a particular circumstance, is another matter.

THE DEVELOPMENT OF E-PROCUREMENT

Large companies have an insatiable thirst for cost reduction, driven by a number of factors:

- They are less agile than their smaller competitors, and need to make up for this partly by offering their customers more competitive prices.
- They have sizeable procurement staffs, who largely need to justify their existence by achieving cost reduction targets.
- They have considerable expenditures on goods and services, which makes their custom highly attractive to vendors.
- They can afford to finance innovative, and possibly speculative, approaches to cost reduction.

In the mid- to late 1990s, a methodology gained increasing acceptance, which was to greatly increase the leverage of buyers. That methodology was e-auctions, or 'reverse auctions'.

In late 1994, Glen Meaken, a 30-year-old executive with General Electric (GE), put forward a proposal which he said would cost US $10 million to develop. He believed the proposed development (e-auctions) could revolutionize procurement in the future. GE turned his proposal down, the equivalent of the Decca Recording Company turning down the Beatles for a recording contract in 1962, with the immortal words 'We don't like their sound. Guitar groups are on the way out.'

Two months later Meaken resigned from GE and founded FreeMarkets, in order to pursue his vision. Five years later, according to _Fortune_ magazine, FreeMarkets had a market capitalization of US $7 billion, and Meaken himself was worth US $750 million.

In the early years the interest of major companies lay almost exclusively in e-auctions, but over time it became apparent that other stages of the buying cycle could also be e-enabled, with numerous benefits – we'll come to this subject later in this chapter.

E-procurement technology has now developed to the point that not only very large companies can take advantage of it. E-auctioning technologies in particular have become somewhat 'commoditized', and the cost of staging events has fallen steadily over the years, making it more feasible for smaller companies to take advantage of it.

For an understanding of quite why e-auctions were so revolutionary and powerful, it might help to have some basic understanding of different types of auctions.

A BRIEF INTRODUCTION TO AUCTIONS – DUTCH, CHINESE, REVERSE, ELECTRONIC, ENGLISH…

The 'Dutch auction' is named after the best-known example, the Dutch tulip auctions. Although in the Netherlands, this type of auction is known as a 'Chinese auction'. Not a lot of people know that. My thanks to Wikipedia.

The Dutch auction is a type of auction where the seller begins with a high asking price, which is lowered until some participating buyer is willing to accept the seller's price, or a predetermined reserve price (the vendor's minimum acceptable price) is reached. The winning participant pays the last announced price. Usually, at least. The seller may have 'auction rules' covering the possibility of price being only one of a number of factors to be considered in the decision-making process. Factors such as a vendor's delivery lead-times and costs, capability, record of innovation – and much more besides – may play a part in the decision-making process.

The 'reverse auction' is a variation on the Dutch auction, in that it is the buyer – not the seller – who is managing the auction process. The buyer sets a price to start the process, and the sellers bid ever-lower prices until a price point is reached at which only one seller (the one who has effectively made the 'final bid') is prepared to conclude a deal.

Where a reverse auction is enabled electronically, over the internet, we have an electronic auction, or 'e-auction'. Typically, the buyer will sit by a computer in his office, while the bidding vendors will sit by computers in *their* offices, which could be located anywhere in the world. The vendors see their own bids and other vendors' bids on their computer screens, but will typically not know the identity of the other vendors. The vendors will make a number of bids over time, the auction duration depending on a number of issues. Most auctions take place within a timeframe of 20 minutes, for the least complex e-auction, up to two days for the most complex.

E-auctions have attracted a great deal of interest in recent years, and some enormous cost savings have been attributed to their use. Claimed savings of 30–50 per cent can usually be attributed to a company seriously market testing a spend area for the first time, so they will probably have done much of the groundwork – such as specification setting – also for the first time. Independent assessments of typical available average savings from repeat e-auction events tend to lie in the region of 11–14 per cent in both the United States and EMEA (Europe, Middle East and Africa).

Finally, for the sake of completeness, in an 'English auction' the auctioneer begins the auction with the reserve price (the lowest acceptable price for the seller), and then takes larger bids from the buyers, until nobody will bid further. The item is then sold to the highest bidder.

Any of these types of auctions may be enabled electronically. For example, when you buy an item through e-Bay, you're involved in an e-enabled English auction, usually with the added twist of the event having a deadline.

E-AUCTION 'DO'S AND DON'TS'

A useful summary of e-auction 'do's and don'ts', which will help ensure a successful e-auction, is shown in Table 9.1 (Eakin, 2001).

EWORLD

25 September 2007, London. The latest 'eWorld Procurement & Supply' forum (www.eworld-purchasing.com), the UK's longest-established and most comprehensive forum for those interested in e-procurement. The programme consisted of more than 20 educational seminars, the latest insights from industry thought-leaders, and a wide range of industry case studies and real-life examples.

Each year since 2001, the event has generated more interest than in the preceding year, and it's no wonder – because e-procurement has been slowly changing the face of procurement in some sectors, and its adoption can only increase.

The excitement created among buyers by e-procurement mainly arises from the increased leverage it gives them – it's now possible to tender requirements to a far larger number of viable vendors, in many countries, than was previously practical. And it has enabled process efficiency improvements.

AN OVERVIEW OF E-PROCUREMENT – THE ABERDEEN GROUP

In business terms, the market for e-procurement services is not mature, and as a result it can be difficult to get an objective view of it, where it's going, and why.

I find the Aberdeen Group (www.aberdeen.com) invaluable for providing insights into the e-procurement marketplace. The Group is

Table 9.1 Ensuring a successful e-auction

	Strategy	Preparation	Event	Follow-up
Buyer	Is this a core competence for my business?	Decide on number of vendors to invite.	Ensure proxy bidding process in place.	Finalize sourcing decision.
	How does this fit with current e-procurement activities?	Provide clear specifications.	Monitor vendor bidding.	Obtain internal approval to decision if required.
	How will this fit with future e-procurement activities?	Ensure there is sufficient market competition – or review approach.	Monitor technology reliability.	Give feedback to all vendors, successful or not.
	What approach to take: full service, supported or self-service?	Gain internal commitment to implement the result.	Monitor bidding tactics. DON'T	Capture knowledge gained.
	What percentage of my spend is e-auctionable?	Develop a robust lot strategy.	Act unethically.	DON'T
	What do I want to achieve by running e-auctions?	Agree evaluation criteria.	Get carried away with the hype – the lowest bid isn't always the best solution.	Underestimate the importance of follow-up.
	What impact will this have on key vendor relationships? DON'T	Set bid decrements.		
	Plan to e-auction everything.	Train vendors.		
		Agree bid format and timing of events.		
		Set clear rules for the event.		
		Set opening price. DON'T		
		Under-inform participating vendors.		
		Plan the event at the wrong time, such as public holidays in the vendors' home countries.		

continued

Table 9.1 *continued*

	Strategy	Preparation	Event	Follow-up
Seller	How much will this impact my sales pipeline? How best to respond? How will this impact my customer's relationships? How will I tailor my approach by customer/product/timing? What do I want to achieve? DON'T Refuse to participate on pricing.	Respond promptly to all the buyer's requests. Undertake all training offered. Pre-prepare initial bid. Consider event-specific strategies. Agree who will be on the bid team. Research your competition. DON'T Ignore offers of help and coaching from the customer or provider.	Have your first bid ready before the start of the event. Submit bids – you have to be in it to win it. DON'T Bid below a sustainable cost. Act unethically.	Provide cost breakdown(s), if requested. If unsuccessful, use benchmark to analyse market price gap. DON'T Ignore lessons learnt – there will almost certainly be a next time.

the leading provider of fact-based research focused on the global technology-driven supply chain. It has established a market-leading position as 'the voice that matters' when it comes to understanding the measurable results being delivered by technology in business.

Aberdeen conducts probing research studies across all aspects of business and technology, with hundreds of companies participating in each research study in order to assure research depth and quality. The research provides specific insight by industry sector, company size, and geography, as well as by business process and technology. Other information about the company:

- It has 394,000+ panel members, and over 2 million readers.
- It has benchmarked over 700,000 locations, and interviewed over 35,000 executives.
- Its research is used by more than 90 per cent of the Fortune 1,000 in over 40 countries.
- It published over 1,200 reports in 2007, which were downloaded over 1 million times.

Andrew Bartolini, Vice President of Global Supply Management Research at Aberdeen, has set an ambitious publishing agenda for 2008. His team plans to publish 30 distinct research reports on Spend Analysis, Sourcing, Contracts, e-Procurement and e-Payables, and a wide range of other topics relevant to procurement professionals.

Aberdeen's benchmark reports are generally available for free to the public for the first eight weeks after they are published. Annual access to the entire Aberdeen research library costs US \$399. For more details, visit www.aberdeen.com/channel/procs.asp.

Aberdeen's Stephen Gold (CEO) and Andrew Bartolini gave keynote speeches at eWorld 2007. Among the interesting findings were the following.

Perception of competitive threats in 2007, among business executives

For all sizes of companies, 'price compression' (pressure to reduce prices to remain competitive) was the number one concern, rating more highly than any of the following (in descending concern order):

- market share erosion;
- people retention;
- feature / functionality differentiation;

- technology obsolescence;
- contractual obstacles;
- intellectual property protection.

Information from chief procurement officers (CPOs)

Table 9.2 summarizes the views of over 200 CPOs from the 2006 'CPO Summit'. The Summit is hosted each November by Aberdeen. Attendees included CPOs from companies such as Toshiba, Bayer, GlaxoSmithKline, IBM and Procter & Gamble. Their combined annual spend responsibility in 2006 was US $1.46 TRILLION.

Aberdeen Group reports

I can thoroughly recommend Aberdeen's research report 'The Advanced Sourcing & Negotiation Benchmark Report: The Art and Science of the Deal', written by Andrew Bartolini. Readers in the EMEA region (Europe, Middle East and Africa) will also be interested in Aberdeen's report 'EMEA: Advanced Sourcing Leads to Tangible Results', available free online at: http://www.aberdeen.com/summary/report/sector_insights/4326-SI-emea.asp.

The first report is some 22 pages long, and full of information that will interest the executive wishing to gain more insight into the opportunities and challenges involved in e-procurement. The following table of contents gives an indication of the report's scope:

Executive Summary
Key business value findings
Implications & analysis
Recommendations for action
Chapter One: Issue at hand
Technology-enabled sourcing
Advanced sourcing primer
An ounce of prevention is worth a pound (or more)
Chapter Two: Key business value findings
No retreat (continue to advance)
Challenges and responses
Sourcing excellence
Chapter Three: Implications and analysis
Process and organization

Table 9.2 CPO operational excellence framework

Measurement criteria	Company type (a)		
	Laggards	Industry average	Best in class
Annual cost savings rate	0–2% Minimal visibility	2–5% Reported with visibility outside of procurement	5% or more Tied to enterprise financial metrics
Procurement ROI %	100–300%	300–700%	700% or more
Spend under management	0–30% Includes common categories (eg indirect supplies)	30–70% Includes core categories (eg raw materials)	70% or more Includes complex categories (eg services)
Budgetary process	Independent of procurement	Based on input from procurement	Procurement is an integral part
Finance relationship	Ad hoc interaction	Regular interaction Reporting to CFO	Continuous interaction Have trust of CFO
Technology utilization	Basic or partial supply management suite	Broad suite, linked to Finance Strong analytics	Full suite Strong linkage to Finance Corporate performance management systems in place

(a) The Aberdeen competitive framework defines companies as falling into one of the three following levels of practices and performance:
Laggards (30%)   practices that are significantly behind the average of the industry
Industry average (50%)   practices that reflect the averages or norm
Best in class (20%)   practices that are the best currently being employed, and significantly superior to the industry norm

Knowledge and technology
Strategic sourcing automation – no pain, strong gains
Pressures, Actions, Capabilities, Enablers (PACE)
Chapter Four: Recommendations for action
Steps to success – laggards
Steps to success – industry average
Next steps – best in class

The Report includes a table comparing companies with regards to a number of e-procurement issues, reproduced as Table 9.3.

E-PROCUREMENT ENABLER 1 – PROCURI INC

As with so many things, one company's problem is another company's opportunity. E-auctions do tend to have a deflationary impact on vendors' prices, but astute vendors will not bury their heads in the sand and hope e-auctioning is going to go away – because it won't. Commercially sharp vendors will see what they can do about the pressure on their margins, and this may include using e-auctions to buy some of their own input goods and services.

Procuri Inc (www.procuri.com) is a major privately held provider of on-demand supply management solutions, whose 300+ customers include Barclays Bank, The Boots Company and UPS. In September 2007 it was acquired by Ariba Inc (www.ariba.com), 'the leading provider of spend management solutions to help companies realize rapid and sustainable bottom line results'.

Tim Minahan is senior vice-president of marketing for Procuri. He is widely regarded as an authority on the subject of e-procurement. He points out that e-auctioning can be good for vendors, and on his online blog www.supplyexcellence.com of 8 August 2006, he outlined 'the 7 myths of e-auctioning'.

Myth 1: e-auctioning is all about lowering prices

False. Thanks to tightening supply markets and maturing sourcing methods, price-only negotiations are less common than they once were. Advanced auctioning capabilities enable buyers to evaluate vendors on a myriad of price and non-price factors, such as lead-times, delivery, quality, and payment terms. Nearly all e-auction users engage in multi-threaded negotiations, such as e-RFI > e-RFP > e-auction.

Table 9.3 E-procurement competitive framework

	Company type		
	Laggards	Industry average	Best in class
Process	No formal enterprise-wide strategic sourcing process. Processes are fully manual. No process visibility. Loose processes employed in certain circumstances.	Some level of process standardization across enterprise. Processes are partially automated. Some visibility into process.	Strategic sourcing processes standardized across enterprise. Uniform processes mapped to technology for complete automation. Process compliance is managed.
Organization	Lack of a formal sourcing organization. Direct and indirect materials procurement may belong in separate organizations.	Sourcing resources decentralized across business units or region. Direct and indirect materials groups often linked.	Formal sourcing organization. Centralized capabilities. Direct and indirect materials groups aligned and closely linked.
Knowledge	No, or limited, e-procurement capabilities. Limited strategic sourcing capabilities.	Sourcing and category competence. Lack of advanced sourcing capabilities. Will leverage external support/ services on occasion.	Sourcing and category proficiency. Platform to leverage expertise. Emerging advanced sourcing capabilities.
Technology	No, or limited, experience with e-sourcing applications. Limited use of other supply management technologies. No advanced sourcing traction.	Some complementary technologies in place. Emerging application expertise to enable the sourcing of more complex categories.	Extended strategic sourcing footprint including spend analysis, e-sourcing, and contracts. Extended advanced sourcing capabilities including external optimization and product lifecycle management applications.

The process enables qualification and evaluation on all attributes of a vendor's capabilities and costs. And many optimization-based sourcing tools allow vendors to offer alternative bundles, or bids that boost their profit margins, and further differentiate their offerings.

Myth 2: e-auctioning is unfair to vendors

Untrue. In most cases e-auctioning introduces greater integrity into the sourcing process than existed in the offline approach. E-auctioning mandates that buyers clearly articulate their selection criteria and business award decision framework to all participating vendors. Vendors go into a negotiation fully knowing how they will be judged, and how the award decision will be made. Any clarifying questions asked by vendors, and resulting answers from the buyer, are available to all vendors to see, further levelling the playing field. This was best summarized by a vice-president of sourcing at Cadbury Schweppes: 'We emphasize fairness and open disclosure on both sides of the sourcing process. We have shut down "backdoors" for internal stakeholders and vendors.'

Myth 3: e-auctioning is unfair to incumbents

No. Competitive incumbents are in a better position to be exposed to more business volume and new business opportunities, particularly considering that any strategic sourcing initiative goes hand-in-hand with a vendor base rationalization effort. Better e-auctioning tools also enable users to incorporate 'transformational' elements that give 'credits' (in the form of switching costs or innovation credits) to well-performing incumbents. As a result, incumbents don't need to be the lowest price bidder in order to win the business. Consider the approach taken by Eastman Kodak: 'We sat down with incumbents to explain why we were using e-auctions, and prepared them with the right strategy and techniques to competitively participate in the event.'

Myth 4: e-auctioning makes it difficult to win new business

On the contrary, e-auctioning dramatically shrinks sourcing cycles. These efficiencies alone enable buyers to negotiate more spend volumes, with more vendors. As noted in the previous example, qualified incumbents delivering a good performance are in a position to expand existing business, and be exposed to new business opportunities. One large manufacturing firm used its e-auctioning strategy to cut the number of MRO (maintenance, repair and operations items) vendors from nearly 2,000 to just 20. Incumbents retaining the business are doing many times the volumes than in the past, and they've added new, more profitable revenue streams, such as integrated supply relationships.

Myth 5: e-auctioning lengthens the sales cycle

There is ample evidence that e-auctioning shortens the sourcing cycle and, hence, sales cycles. And as an old boss of mine would say, 'In a sales cycle, getting to "no" fast can be as valuable as getting to yes.' His point was that quickly getting to 'no' enables you to focus your salesforce on the opportunities they can win.

Myth 6: e-auctioning burdens vendors with new cost, technology and resource requirements

Wrong again. There is compelling evidence that e-auctioning can reduce vendors' costs. A recent study from the University of North Texas found that vendors could reduce their 'cost of sales' (salesperson commissions, advertising etc) using e-auctions.

Myth 7: e-auctioning eliminates buyer–vendor relationships

I recently asked a supply management executive at a major life sciences company how he was able to drive such aggressive use of e-auctions. He replied 'I tell vendors, "If you believe your customer relationship is all about negotiating, then you don't have a relationship".' Now this isn't just rhetoric. Many companies have begun partnering with vendors to remove cost from the entire supply chain. New multi-tier sourcing, co-sourcing, and buy–sell approaches are being embraced by a wide range of enterprises (notably in the aerospace, automotive and high-tech sectors) looking to gain better visibility into costs and risks inherent in the sub-tier supply chain, and to aggregate spend volumes and remove costs from the total supply chain.

CASE STUDY: THE BOOTS COMPANY
SAVES £3.5 MILLION PA THROUGH E-AUCTIONS

The Boots Company plc is Europe's leading pharmacy-led health and beauty group. A few years ago, the company faced a number of challenges:

- It needed a quick and effective method to standardize and streamline global sourcing practices;
- It required a solution to make it easy for vendors to receive and collaborate in electronic information exchanges (requests for proposals and the like), and e-auction projects;
- It wanted to simultaneously increase vendor participation in the sourcing process, and decrease sourcing administration.

Boots selected a solution from Procuri, due to its extensive features, its ease of use, training, and support to maximize vendor participation (Boots' vendors' staff received training from Procuri, at no cost to the vendors).

The results of the initiative were impressive. In the space of only two months Boots conducted 18 e-auctions, covering a total expenditure of some £13.0m pa, and negotiated savings worth £3.5m pa (27 per cent).

Tim Minahan of Procuri also reported the case of the ITT Corporation, a global company that provides products and services in many markets, including equipment for water and wastewater treatment, and other industrial products.

In May 2007, in London, ITT's Jessica Dunlop, e-auctioning and strategic purchasing manager, gave an 'encore performance' outlining how new approaches had helped ITT overcome the mounting pressures of rising global competition and turmoil in the telecommunications industry, one of ITT's core businesses. She told a sold-out audience of UK purchasing managers how the telecom crash forced ITT to cut its telecom-related workforce in half between 2001 and 2002. At the same time, 70 per cent of the telecom supply base moved to the Far East, particularly China.

Dunlop outlined how ITT used a number of e-auctioning-enabled processes – including the use of total-cost-based e-auctions – to drive repeatable annual double-digit cost improvements for machines components over several years. 'We were surprised at our ability to drive such large savings with each subsequent auction,' she stated.

She proceeded to give her audience 'candid tips' on how to maximize the benefits from e-auctions, and what pitfalls to avoid. Here are just some of her recommendations.

Lotting makes all the difference

'We realized we don't have to bundle all our business into a single auction to get the best price. The vendors will identify what meets their capabilities and provide the best price.' It is important to note that, regardless of the lot structure, ITT does not typically require vendors to bid on all items.

Four is the magic number

In its first e-auction for machined parts, ITT included only three vendors. Dunlop said this number didn't provide sufficient competition to encourage aggressive bidding.

Better trained vendors make more competitive offers

Dunlop also said that, early on, many vendors were confused about the auction approach, bidding aggressively to be the lowest price, even though ITT had said it would award the business on multiple factors to get the lowest total cost. 'One vendor bid away all his margin, which is not a sustainable or preferable business for him or us,' she explained. ITT has since placed a strong emphasis on educating vendors on the selection criteria and business award strategy, to ensure competitive (and sustainable) bids.

Clearly define the rules of engagement – before the auction begins

In one auction, a winning vendor later tried to place conditions on its offered pricing after the event closed. To guard against such post-event bartering, ITT now uses pre-qualifying gateways and 'knockout questions' to ensure that vendors agree to all conditions prior to the auction, and to avoid any surprises or disputes after award.

Beware of sour grapes

After its second auction, ITT noticed that one vendor that was well out of the running kept placing bids to trigger extension periods, and force other more qualified and competitive vendors to continue to bid down their price. ITT eventually closed out the auction and later revoked the vendor's auction privileges. Dunlop advises constant monitoring of auction events to discourage such tactics.

Spending time with losers can create great winners

ITT discovered that telling vendors why they hadn't won the business could provide much-needed motivation (and insight) for self-improvement. 'We've had vendors go out and buy new machinery or start joint ventures in Asia, and come back much more competitive, to win our business,' said Dunlop.

Involve Asian vendors whenever possible

ITT has also tracked a correlation between bidding activity and the participation of Asian vendors, particularly those from China. 'Involving Asian vendors in an auction can help force local vendors to be more competitive.'

E-PROCUREMENT ENABLER 2 – BRAVOSOLUTION

Steve Ellesmere of BravoSolution (www.bravosolution.com) gave an interesting presentation at eWorld 2007, on 'The Reality of Implementing e-Procurement'. First, a profile of the company:

- leading international provider of e-procurement solutions;
- combining professional expertise and technological excellence in the area of procurement;
- offices in London, Rome, Madrid, Paris and Shanghai;
- client portfolio comprises over 300 leading and international organizations, in 18 countries;
- over 85,000 vendors from 80 countries involved in e-procurement process;
- advanced e-procurement technology available in seven languages;
- online negotiations support services available in 20 languages;

- over 70,000 online negotiations managed, totalling over £25 billion of spend;
- average cash savings in the private sector is 15 per cent. Private sector clients include Hilton Hotels, Vodafone and EDF;
- average cash savings in the public sector is 20 per cent. Public sector clients include the NHS, the Home Office and the BBC.

The company cites five key business rationales for using e-procurement:

- Cycle time – you can conclude your sourcing initiatives in the quickest time possible.
- Focus – you can free your buyers' time and energy so they can focus more on value-adding areas.
- Governance – you can keep track of all decision making activities and policies, plus ensure compliance.
- Risk – you can reduce risk and ensure appropriate goods and services are procured from reliable vendors.
- Cost savings – you can improve the performance of your negotiations in the short and long term.

Ellesmere then outlined his company's view on what makes a 'best-in-class enterprise e-procurement platform', a cycle with the following stages:

1. E-spend analysis – monitor spend;
2. E-advertising – advertise opportunities to potential vendors;
3. Low-cost country sourcing – identify sources of comparative advantage;
4. E-vendor management – assess vendor capabilities;
5. E-RFX/e-tendering – get quotes;
6. E-evaluation – evaluate proposals;
7. E-auction – negotiate;
8. E-reporting – analyse and control;
9. E-contract management – measure performance.

Ellesmere presented the following case studies where his company had acted as the 'e-auction enabler'.

CASE STUDY: HOTEL COMPANY FORECASTS £621,000 COST SAVINGS, AFTER AN E-AUCTION FOR PAPER NAPKINS AND PLACEMATS

Company: major international hotel company
Category: paper napkins and placemats
Annual spend: £690,000
Summary: £621,000 cost savings are forecast over three years after an e-auction reduced prices by 25 per cent. A further 5 per cent saving is being realized through lower inbound supply chain costs.

Background

The company was moving towards global strategic sourcing, though the implementation of a regional procurement organization, directed by a central team. Consolidation of the inbound supply chain had been achieved through third-party logistics providers, deployed in all regions. The central team approached BravoSolution because they needed to:

- gain visibility of spend globally;
- gain control of sourcing activities globally;
- improve the productivity of the entire sourcing process;
- achieve a fully auditable sourcing process;
- achieve best value in all sourcing activities.

BravoSolution recommended that a series of pilot online tenders should be implemented, to enable key users in their procurement organization to gain hands-on experience, to demonstrate the productivity benefits of e-procurement, and to drive cost savings through spend aggregation. They further recommended that sources of supply in India and China should be explored.

The first pilot tender was conducted for paper napkins and placemats. They were being sourced at a country level across UK and Europe, including a number of East European countries. Local vendors were delivering direct to hotels.

Action taken

Specifications and volumes were confirmed, and a long list of potential vendors established. Vendors were invited to register on the sourcing portal and complete the online RFI. Auto-scoring tools in the system allowed the initial vendor list of 12 to be reduced to 7. These were invited to the e-RFQ, and requested to submit samples based on the specifications provided. Again an element of auto-scoring greatly reduced the time taken to evaluate vendor responses. Following evaluation of the samples and the non-price elements of the vendors' responses, six vendors were invited to a 'best value' reverse e-auction. The auction included eight lots, and permitted ranking on the basis of total scores, ie price and non-price issues. Vendors provided both FOB and CIF prices, to enable the company to compare the option of vendor delivery to the logistics platform versus company collection using its nominated carrier.

Outcome

A UK-based vendor was selected to supply the entire UK and European volumes, into two logistics platforms. Savings of 25 per cent of annual spend were forecast over the three-year contract. By supplying the product through consolidation centres, distribution cost savings and process efficiencies in the inbound supply chain were also achieved, equivalent to a further 5 per cent of the former cost prices. By using e-procurement tools, the entire process from specification to award was reduced from four months to two, and a complete audit trail of all activities was recorded. The company has decided to extend the project to other categories.

CASE STUDY: THE NATIONAL HEALTH SERVICE (NHS) SAVES OVER £100 MILLION ON TEMPORARY STAFF THROUGH A THREE DAY LONG E-AUCTION

Organization: National Health Service (NHS)
Category: Temporary staff
Annual spend: £420 million
Summary: A three day long e-auction, engaging 176 vendors, led to new three-year contracts with a reduced number of vendors. Savings of over £100 million are forecast over the new contract lifetimes.

Background

The NHS negotiates framework agreements for the provision of goods and services, with an annual procurement spend in the region of £4.5 billion, managed by 340 staff at four sites. The organization had been actively seeking a public sector compliant e-sourcing solution for some time. E-sourcing was seen as an essential component of the organization's restructuring process, as it offered an opportunity to implement procurement best practice across the organization. An e-tendering solution was required to enable staff to source the next wave of framework agreements as efficiently as possible. E-auction functionality was also required, to deliver direct savings through increased vendor competition.

Action taken

The NHS adopted the e-tendering element of BravoSolution's e-sourcing solution. This web-based technology, securely hosted and supported by BravoSolution, facilitates buyer and vendor interaction throughout the tender process. It handles online tenders both above and below OJEU (_Official Journal of the European Union_) thresholds, and includes built-in e-auction functionality.

The organization launched its e-tendering portal in July 2005, and the results have been impressive. Since the launch, all new NHS contracts have been negotiated via the service. As a result, within the first six months of the service going live, more than 100 tenders were published, with over 1,500 vendors participating. The e-tendering service has allowed the exchange of nearly 2,000 tender documents and enabled around 20,000 automated communications, during this initial period. The majority of these interactions between the organization and its vendors would previously have been performed manually, by e-mail or using hard-copy document exchange.

The organization recently conducted one of the largest e-auctions worldwide, offering three-year contracts for the provision of temporary staffing services, for a total estimated value of £1.26 billion. The e-auction was conducted in several lots over three days, with the participation of 176 employment agencies from across the UK. It registered an unprecedented 60,000 bids.

Outcome

The organization is forecasting savings of over £100 million as a result of the e-auction, the number of agencies has been reduced, and the administration burden of the organization has been reduced. The resultant time savings for the NHS have been considerable, leading to significant performance and productivity improvements.

E-PROCUREMENT ENABLER 3 – VENDIGITAL

Another interesting presentation at eWorld 2007 was that given by Adrian Griffiths of Vendigital (www.vendigital.com). The company describes itself on its website as follows:

> As a world leading sourcing and market purchasing specialist, Vendigital connects its industrial and business customers to the global market place. The company delivers rapid business

improvements and dramatic cost savings, through enhanced purchasing processes, and access to new supply chain options. Vendigital is a pioneer in the use of purchasing technology, and its highly skilled team delivers average cost savings of 26 per cent.

Vendigital's strategic whilst practical approach to cost reduction programmes, specialist market tenders, and e-auctions, through to category management services, consistently delivers eye-catching results – helping clients to increase profits, and improve supply chains. Established in 2000, Vendigital has global reach through offices in the UK, US and Germany.

Vendigital's team of procurement professionals and multilingual market researchers enables them to 'headhunt' optimal vendors, and to conduct business in 19 languages. They have tendered over £1 billion of goods and services for clients, and generated average savings of 26 per cent.

Vendigital work with someone well known to the procurement community, Professor Richard Lamming, who contributes the 'latest thinking' which feeds into Vendigital's solutions. Professor Lamming is recognized as an international expert in contemporary developments in procurement, strategic sourcing, supply chain relationships and the implications of e-commerce. He has an engineering background, and had practical experience of purchasing in the manufacturing sector before becoming an academic in the 1980s. His doctoral work focused on innovation in manufacturing supply chains, and his research at MIT led to the development of the supply concepts associated with lean production. After 12 years in the School of Management at the University of Bath, where he was founder and first director of the Centre for Research in Strategic Purchasing and Supply (CRISPS), he moved to the University of Southampton in 2004, to become director of the School of Management.

CASE STUDY: VENDIGITAL CLIENT GAINS ACCESS TO A MORE APPROPRIATE VENDOR, AND REDUCES COSTS BY 25 PER CENT

The first case study presented at eWorld concerned Vendigital's work with Vetco Grey, a century-old company with global brand awareness in upstream oil and gas development. Vetco Grey has annual revenues in excess of US $1.6 billion, and more than 11,000 employees in 33 countries. It merged with General Electric in March 2007.

The spend area in question was that of hydraulic manifolds, a component used within drilling equipment on the sea bed, when drilling for oil and gas. Vetco Grey's customers clearly work in very demanding conditions, and they look to Vetco Grey for innovative solutions. Vetco Grey has a very capable in-house engineering function, but much of the innovation sought by customers actually comes from Vetco Grey's vendors.

Vetco Grey identified a number of problems with regard to hydraulic manifolds:

- Customers require them at short notice, as breaks in production are very costly.
- There are five main designs, and 50 variants.
- The incumbent vendor struggled with quality and lead-times.
- The task of finding a new vendor was daunting.

At which point Vendigital entered the scene. They used their expertise to fully explore supply market options, leading to the following sequence of events:

1. 227 potential vendors were identified and analysed;
2. 69 met the size and experience criteria, and were engaged in discussions;
3. 32 were shortlisted and proceeded to the detailed tender stage;
4. five eventually took part in an auction to establish prices;
5. final vendors were visited and vendor quality audits carried out;
6. Newburgh Engineering Ltd selected as new vendor.

Now the key reasons that Newburgh Engineering was chosen were: their manufacturing operations were more appropriate for the manifolds being bought by Vetco Grey; and their considerable technical expertise led to innovative, superior solutions. The results were shorter lead-times, 25 per cent lower prices, and improved quality.

Intriguingly, following market testing of other spend areas, the original vendor ended up with far more business than they had started with, through selling products that were more within their area of core competence.

One of the learning points from the case study is that unless companies make a very thorough trawl of the marketplace, they may well fail to locate the one or two potential vendors whose business offering would align extremely well with their own needs, in areas such as potential for offering innovative solutions.

As is so often the case with e-procurement, the story doesn't end there. Newburgh Engineering, the vendor that won the Vetco Grey contract, itself turned to Vendigital to reduce its own costs. And so the benefits of e-procurement were reaped down the supply chain.

CASE STUDY: NEWBURGH ENGINEERING APPLIES VENDIGITAL EXPERTISE TO ITS OWN SUPPLY CHAIN

Newburgh Engineering Ltd made 15 per cent cost savings on its £850,000 pa spend on duplex stainless steel grades, using the sourcing and market purchasing expertise of Vendigital. This significant saving was achieved in a raw material market that had been rising for the past 24 months, a trend which was predicted to continue with the ongoing strength in demand, and volatile nickel prices.

'Vendigital's expertise enabled us not only to reduce costs, but also to protect our stainless steel costs for the foreseeable future,' said Matthew Jewitt, marketing manager at Newburgh. 'It's vital that we maintain a competitive price. One of our most important customers is Vetco Grey. We provide high-specification steel valves and kits for Vetco Grey's onshore and offshore oil and gas drilling and production equipment. By sharing the benefits of these savings with Vetco Grey, we can add further value to this relationship.'

Vendigital undertook a detailed assessment of the stainless steel plate, bar and forging market within Western and Eastern Europe. Owing to the limited supply options available, Vendigital focused on restructuring the way Newburgh purchased its raw materials, and five different sourcing scenarios were presented. Following a detailed assessment of individual vendor capabilities, Newburgh opted for the best-value proposition, which involved moving from a single source to a dual supply.

Matthew Jewitt added, 'This is the first time we've worked with a company like Vendigital, and the experience has been extremely positive. Vendigital became an extension of our own procurement department. They helped us to adopt a more strategic approach to the way we source our materials. And we plan to invite Vendigital's highly professional team back again when the contract comes to an end. I anticipate that this will ensure the renegotiations have an equally positive outcome.'

10

Organizational issues

In buying mode, most executives are money-shredding machines,
and most organizations are money-shredding factories.

(Andrew Heslop, procurement consultant)

This chapter contains:

- Politics.
- Buying development stages.
- Approaches to buying.
- Building buying capacity and capability: employees, interim managers, consultants.
- Maximizing the value derived from external experts.
- Matching buyer personalities/aptitudes to tasks.
- Buyer motivation and incentivization.
- Individual roles, responsibilities and authorities.
- Buyers' product knowledge.
- Buyers' contract law knowledge.
- Buyers' competence development.
- Performance measurement and reporting.
- Ethics.

Buying in general, and cost reduction in particular, obviously takes place within an organizational context. Organizational issues can either help or hinder cost reduction efforts, so it makes sense to take them seriously.

POLITICS

Whenever I am considering whether or not to take on a new assignment, a key question I always ask myself is: 'What is the likely level of organizational motivation in respect of cost reduction?' In all organizations there are middle and senior executives who will try to thwart cost reduction efforts – overtly or covertly, sometimes both. Such realities are often termed the 'politics' of the situation.

I once worked for a company that had numerous operations around the UK. The chief executive had charged me with high (but attainable) cost reduction targets, but would do nothing to persuade or oblige middle or senior managers to cooperate with me. I was trying to negotiate a country-wide deal on capital equipment, and a number of local managers were cooperating fully with me, providing data and so on. But sufficient numbers of local managers refused to cooperate with me, which meant that I could not offer potential vendors the sales volumes required for an advantageous contract.

Some of the managers said they needed to select their vendors, as they were responsible for their site's performance – despite the fact that the company had a number of large competitors, which had adopted a centralized approach to buying such equipment many years previously, to great advantage. I had worked for one myself and was responsible for this particular area, and I understood it intimately. But the chief executive would simply not get involved to the extent required, and I had no option but to resign.

The only point of relating this story is to illustrate that some organizations simply aren't sufficiently motivated to make the changes required to deliver cost reduction – in that case, local managers' morale was deemed more important than cost reduction. And in some cases, senior executives' determination crumbles at the first sign of colleagues' opposition. Which is why the most successful cost reduction programmes often take place within organizations that recognize they have no choice but to undertake them – 'if we don't do this now, we won't be around for the short term, never mind the long term'.

Organizations are often their own worst enemies – their structures, processes, recruitment policies and politics all 'build in' cost. Which is just one of the reasons why 'lean' small organizations can often not only take on their larger competitors, but trounce them.

Within a given market sector, even organizations of a similar size can differ greatly with respect to how seriously they take procurement. If the procurement team is seen as a motley collection of low-level paper shufflers, that's what they'll remain, until the organization decides to move forward. Which brings us neatly on to the next section.

BUYING DEVELOPMENT STAGES

A number of buying development stages within organizations are recognized, as illustrated in Table 10.1. Broadly speaking, the larger the organization, the more geographically dispersed its operations and the larger the proportion of turnover attributable to third-party spend, the further to the right of the table one might expect to find individual organizations. But in practice, most organizations are far less well developed in buying terms than you might expect. I believe there are a number of reasons for this:

- a lack of understanding, within the broad business community, of the potential benefits – including cost reduction – that flow from professional buying practices;
- an unwillingness to pay the remuneration packages expected by talented buying professionals, maybe because they appear excessive when compared to professionals in other functions – but of course, this completely ignores the point that buying professionals will typically save their organizations many times more than they cost;
- a shortage of talented buying professionals willing to switch employers;
- executive resistance to relinquishing some of their power in the selection and management of vendors;
- lack of a history of professional buying in some sectors, so there's not a competitive advantage issue – at least, not until one or more companies in the sector decide to professionalize their buying.

APPROACHES TO BUYING

There are a range of approaches to buying, as illustrated in Table 10.2. In some ways, the approaches mirror the buying development stages. That is, the larger the organization, the more geographically dispersed its operations and the larger the proportion of turnover attributable to third-party spend, the further down the table one might expect to find

Table 10.1 Buying development stages within organizations

Parameter	1 – Basic	2 – Cost focused	3 – Coordinated	4 – Strategic
Company size	Small	Moderate	Large, probably national or regional	Very large, probably international
Staffing	No full-time buyers	One or a few individual(s) starting to spend most of their time buying	Trained buyers	Head of Buying with a sizeable buying staff
Ownership of the cost reduction challenge	None	Limited to very few individuals	Numerous individuals, mainly within the buying function	Many individuals formally charged with the role, both in and outside the buying function
Policies and procedures	None	A few, eg a sign-off-level policy	Moderately well developed	Highly developed
Buying systems	None	Modest, and paper-based eg purchase orders	Increasingly electronic	Almost all electronic, including authorizations
Quality of information on expenditure	Very poor	Poor to moderate	Good	Excellent
Number of vendors (with respect to the company size in its sector)	Variable	Moderate to large	Moderate	Small

continued

Table 10.1 *continued*

Parameter	1 – Basic	2 – Cost focused	3 – Coordinated	4 – Strategic
Contract terms	Buying on the vendors' terms	Starting to buy on own terms in a few areas	Buying on own terms in numerous key areas	Buying on own terms for most key spend areas
Approach to cost management	Highly reactive if any approach at all	Some effort to contain costs, eg 3 quotations for large commitments	Sustained effort to reduce costs in major spend areas	Sustained and structured drive to reduce costs across the whole buying portfolio
Cross-functional team-working on buying	None	Very limited	Limited to major spend areas	Sustained approach
Recognition of the importance of the buying cycle concept	None	Very limited	Moderate in a few major spend areas	Strong
Recognition of the importance of the total cost of ownership	None	Very limited	Moderate in a few major spend areas	Strong
Use of consultants and/or interims to boost performance	None	Limited	Limited to moderate	Variable, from limited to considerable

Table 10.2 Approaches to buying

Approach	Advantages	Disadvantages
No central negotiation of any spend areas	Local management motivated by control	Lost opportunity to leverage overall spend. Poor use of local management time. Increased commercial and risk exposure.
Central negotiation of some minor spend areas eg stationery	Fairly uncontroversial, so opposition will be weak	Lost opportunity to leverage major areas for greater impact
Central negotiation of some major spend areas	Commercial benefits if carried out well	Few people with required buying expertise. Active senior level support required, or local management and vendors will undermine. Local management resentment over loss of power. Likely to be a slow process. Contracts likely to be poorly drafted.
Introduction of full-time buying resource	Commercial and contractual benefits. Moderately fast progress, particularly if individuals have experience of the key spend areas	Few people with the required spend area experience. Active senior level support required, or local management and vendors may undermine. Local management resentment over loss of power. Return on investment will take some time, and may decline over time after some 'big wins' are delivered.
Introduction of interim managers, and/or consultants	Fast transfer of expertise into organization. Interim managers and consultants will get through organizational barriers more rapidly than employees	Need to avoid reliance in the longer term. May need sophisticated management. May be costly.

individual organizations. But again, we find that most organizations' approaches to buying are often far less sophisticated than one might expect, and for much the same reasons.

BUILDING BUYING CAPACITY AND CAPABILITY: EMPLOYEES, INTERIM MANAGERS, CONSULTANTS

Table 10.3 outlines the key issues to be considered in this area, with respect to the options of existing staff redeployment and external recruitment. Many professional buyers are of the view that extensive training and hands-on buying experience are vital to success in a buying role, at all levels. However, there is a school of thought, gaining more adherents over time, that individuals from other disciplines – with the required attitudes and beliefs – can make a strong contribution after having been taught the basics of buying, such as I am outlining in this book.

Employees

Companies wishing to recruit professional buyers have a number of options, including online recruitment, press advertising and recruitment agencies. Some of the agencies specialize in buyer recruitment, while some also cover related disciplines such as logistics.

Companies in the UK have the benefit of an excellent independent guide to salaries and remuneration of professional buyers in the UK, namely the Purcon Salary Study, produced for many years by Purcon Ltd (www.purcon.co.uk). At the time of writing, the latest biannual survey is available for only £150.00 (exc VAT). The study gives comprehensive details of the ranges of salary packages, bonuses and company car ownership of buyers in the UK, in line with:

- role seniority;
- company size;
- region of the UK;
- industrial sector;
- qualifications.

An excerpt from the report is provided in Appendix 7.

Table 10.3 Approaches to staffing a buying function

Issue	Existing staff redeployment	External recruitment
Expertise	The selected individual(s) will require extensive competence development, to acquire the buying expertise required for such a difficult role.	Individuals with high levels of expertise can be recruited, with the right remuneration package. But there is a perennial shortage of the most able candidates, many of whom prefer the variety, challenge and reward of consultancy or interim work, to employment.
Experience	Likely to have in-depth understanding of how the company really works. May have some familiarity with a number of key spend areas. Unlikely to know of, or be equipped to introduce, innovative approaches.	Should have experience of major change management with regards to buying. Should have experience of the major spend areas. The need to learn how the company really works will result in a 'learning curve'.
Credibility	The right individual may have high personal credibility, if no purchasing credibility.	The right individual will have high buying credibility, but personal credibility will have to be earned.
Cost	Likely to be modest.	Likely to be high – a substantial package will probably be required to attract candidates with the required intellect, expertise, experience and drive.
Risks	Unless and until well trained, existing staff may make decisions that could impact adversely on company profitability over time, or lead to litigation – major errors could even threaten the company's survival.	Possibility of a poor alignment of buying activities with company needs, without extensive and ongoing dialogue with senior company executives.
Speed of impact	Likely to be slow, and there will be a natural reluctance to challenge the 'existing order', which would mean antagonizing colleagues, possibly of long standing. Need for highly visible senior-level commitment and support.	Likely to be fast. Ongoing need for highly visible senior-level commitment and support.

Interim managers

The use of interim managers has grown strongly over recent years, and with good reason. They are highly experienced executives who can 'hit the ground running' and, with a short termination period – often just a week – they are highly incentivized to deliver strong and visible value, on a day-by-day basis.

There are a number of companies engaged in the provision of interim buyers, often alongside their work in other disciplines. An internet search will find a number, but I can strongly recommend two from personal experience, Odgers Ray & Berndtson (www.odgers.com), and Impact Executives (www.impactexecutives.com). Impact Executives makes a very lucid case for the use of interim managers on its website, from which the following is drawn, with the company's kind permission.

Why use interim managers?

Companies often use interim managers when they are in need of immediate hands-on support through periods of rapid growth, or loss of key personnel. Impact Executives' interim managers provide benefits to companies because they are:

- flexible: and available much more quickly than permanent staff;
- widely experienced: with the senior authority and expertise necessary to see projects through – bringing relevant business experience that companies aren't easily able to access, and supporting the internal team in acquiring new skills;
- more focused, results-oriented and productive than permanent staff: they are able to see a project right through to completion;
- more cost-effective than permanent staff: research shows they can provide up to 31 per cent better value for money (see Table 10.4);
- less risky than permanent staff: their termination period will be much shorter.

When should you use interim managers?

Interim managers have proved time and again to be a highly effective, immediate solution for organizations of all sizes which are looking to rapidly improve their performance. Interim managers are crucial when organizations experience:

- re-engineering: BPR or organizational restructure requires an experienced manager to drive through a programme;

Table 10.4 Cost comparison, full-time employees versus interim managers

	Full-time employee	Interim manager
Proportion of time spent on primary activities (planning, implementation, measurement) = A	60%	90%
Proportion of time spent on secondary activities (internal meetings, research, professional development, politics, staff management, travel) = B	40%	10%
Annual working days	215	215
Annual costs	VISIBLE COSTS Salary / bonus £120,000 Benefits (health + car) £6,000 Payroll taxes £14,868 Pension + life assurance £18,000 OTHER COSTS Staff expenses £1,000 Training £750 Recruitment fee (a) £10,000 RISK OF EMPLOYMENT Redundancy / severance (b) £26,478 TOTAL COSTS = C £197,096	215 days @ £800pd = £172,000 = D
Value delivered to the company = cost of time spent on primary spent on primary activities = C × A / 100 (full-time employee), D × A / 100 (interim manager)	£118,258	£154,800
Value delivery premium, interim manager v full-time employee		+31%

Calculation based on 25% of salary / bonus, apportioned over 3 years.
Calculation based on 6 months' notice, apportioned over 3 years.
© Impact Executives 2005

- rapid growth or product launch: a company needs to expand into a new market sector quickly;
- crisis or change: the organization is going through a crisis or period of major change, merger, acquisition or management buy-out, and needs immediate, experienced help;
- recruitment gaps: there will be a long gap in the recruitment of a new senior executive, and the organization needs a 'safe pair of hands' until a permanent replacement is found;
- loss of key executives: a key manager is going to be absent through illness or maternity, paternity or compassionate leave.

Interim managers help companies who need:

- to improve the bottom line: someone who can quickly identify where profits can be enhanced or savings made – and implement the changes required;
- quick results: a project has been delayed, and needs to be kick-started by a manager with the authority and experience to ensure project recovery;
- flexibility: a business needs hands-on managerial support to maintain a key team or project, but doesn't want to incur permanent recruitment costs, particularly if it is going through restructuring or major change;
- new skills: there is a need for 'someone who has done this before' and the relevant skills or experience are lacking internally;
- hands-on help: a start-up company needs experience and hands-on help to get the business up and running, but doesn't have the resources to employ permanent staff members.

But for the vigilance of their superiors, junior employees would happily divide their working day between idly surfing the internet for fun, and sending trivial e-mails to each other. This, at any rate, is the suspicion harboured by many senior managers.

While above this kind of frivolity, senior employees are quite capable of compromising their own productivity. Particularly during times of relative stability and growth, senior management will all too easily default to spending disproportionate time on what might be described as 'corporate activity'. At the more excusable end of the scale, this includes time lavished on endless internal meetings, attendance at conferences of questionable usefulness, and wallowing in the sea of internal communications that their positions throw at them.

At its most negative, it includes the machinations of internal politics. Much energy can be expended in competing for advancement up the career ladder, or in demonstrating indispensability to those above. Some executives become so blinkered that they lose all sense of the real value they should provide for their employer, and start to treat their position as a fiefdom to be defended at all costs.

When management layers are shed after a takeover, it's this 'layer of fat' that usually gets removed first. But, as prevention is better than cure, top-level managers are starting to consider ways in which the build-up of this 'fat layer' can be avoided in the first place.

An obvious option is the interim manager, a highly qualified professional brought in to oversee a particular project, paid solely on the basis of their time and achievements. Historically many organizations have eschewed this route, their prejudice mainly based on the assumption that an interim manager is likely to be more expensive than a permanent manager, regardless of whatever qualities they bring to the party.

This is not borne out by the facts, and research by Impact Executives indicates the opposite. Typically, an interim manager will cost around £800 per day, compared with around £120,000 pa for an equivalent senior full-time employee.

But this £800 goes a long way. To begin with, there are no extra payroll costs, such as National Insurance or health schemes. Interim executives are not provided with car benefits, pension plans, or the panoply of executive ancillary extras. And since they are paid by the day, they have to add value by the day, giving their performance an edge often lacked by someone safe in a lengthy contract. Most hiring strategies adopted by companies ignore the real financial impact of recruitment, both in terms of time and money, as well as other expenses such as training, holidays, maternity/paternity leave and travel.

One finance director at a major listed company said: 'I am amazed at the hidden costs of recruitment and severance. Most executive packages will cost the company an additional 20 per cent on the annual payroll, due to these two factors. Even finance directors do not realize the hidden cost of employing executives until they are involved with a downsizing or restructuring. With the changes in employment patterns, we are experiencing these costs on a three-year cycle.'

One obvious strength of an interim is the speed at which they can be employed, and conversely their deployment. On just a week's notice, an interim executive can be terminated, should their project face an early demise. No induction period is required to make them productive, nor training needed to bring them up to speed. This all comes with the interim package, on day one.

Furthermore, as the interim manager is outside the normal office politics, you won't find them jockeying for favour with the chief executive. They have no pet projects to defend, and no motivation to sit in endless meetings, where the minutiae of corporate processes are picked over in detail.

Without emotional attachment, they can spot projects and initiatives that have become sacred cows to full-time managers, and will have no compunction about shooting them where necessary. Where inventory needs reducing, cash flow increasing, labour costs cutting and unproductive sites shutting down, the impartial interim can play a dispassionate and professional role.

And as their diary is at the company's disposal, their days will not be clogged by conferences, seminars or industry think-tank meetings. They spend little time at airports, on trains, or in transit between the different divisions of a distributed enterprise. Their role is tight and focused, their schedule lean and spare.

Interim managers can help make your company agile, by saving on the need to staff up in advance for anticipated growth. Instead you can reach out for the instant expertise of the interim at the precise point of need. Interims will make you flexible too, by maximizing value creation, at the same time as minimizing costs.

As a supplement to the existing management team, a replacement for a senior manager or a leader of a new project, the interim executive is an invaluable weapon in the battle to maximize competitiveness.

But what about cost effectiveness? Table 10.4 demonstrates that a 'typical' interim manager may be expected to deliver 31 per cent more 'value for money' than a 'typical' senior full-time employee.

Consultants

In the area of buying, as in many other areas, the UK is fortunate in having experienced consultants, highly capable of designing and executing cost reduction programmes. Most consultants work under one of three operating models, and Table 10.5 outlines the key advantages and disadvantages of each model.

An issue meriting particular attention is how to reward procurement consultants. If the prime focus of an assignment is cost reduction, a high return on investment (ROI) may be expected – often 10:1 or more for sole consultants working on large budgets. That is, for every £1.00 you pay the consultant, you may expect £10.00 of cost savings to follow. The ROI will generally be smaller with specialist consultancies, and smaller still with large multi-offering consultancies. So to what extent should you consider negotiating 'percentage of cost savings' contracts, ie contracts where some or all of the consultant's reward is a proportion of cost savings?

Table 10.5 Comparison between different consultancy operating models

	Sole consultant	Specialist consultancy	Multi-offering international consultancy
Key advantages of the model	Very cost effective. Likely to offer a bespoke solution rather than 'off the shelf'.	Highly cost effective. Consultants benefit from exposure to the experience and expertise of colleagues.	Cost effective. Access to plenty of bright people at short notice. International scope. Multi-disciplined. Consultants benefit from exposure to the experience and expertise of colleagues.
Key disadvantages of the model	Limited to experience and expertise of just one person, although that might be perfectly appropriate for particular requirements.	Unlikely to be able to resource a major assignment at short notice. Unlikely to offer significant international scope.	Costly for a number of reasons: partners are highly-paid salesmen but not generally operationally active; inexperienced consultants are developed at the client's expense; consultants have to be paid for, even when not actively fee-earning; expensive overheads (eg offices in prime city locations) need to be paid for.

This is a difficult area. On the one hand you want to incentivize the consultant, but you equally need to recognize that high ROIs are a natural outcome of procurement assignments which focus on cost reduction. There is also the question of exactly what constitutes a 'cost saving', not always an easy matter. There are numerous tales of procurement consultants claiming certain cost savings, where the client is of the view that the cost savings would have been delivered by themselves anyway in due course, or the consultant's role in the savings delivery has been small or moderate. For such reasons, the client–consultant relationship may deteriorate. In general my advice would be to pay consultants a professional daily rate, and have only a small part of their income derived from sharing cost savings. This will also temper their potential willingness to take risks with your business, simply to deliver cost savings in the short term. The consultant will wish to leave the assignment with their reputation intact or enhanced.

Sole consultants

These are generally individuals with a strong track record, whose level of experience and expertise enables them to make a living, often a very good one. They are generally prepared to work as interims as well as consultants, and often belong to formal or informal networks of independent experts.

Employees of specialist consultancies

The UK has for many years had a number of specialist buying consultancies, which these days are likely to market themselves as 'procurement consultancies'. An example is ADR International (www.adr-international.com), which played a key role in SmithKline Beecham's cost reduction programme in the 1990s. The story is related in Appendix 6.

Employees of full service consultancies

In this category come the major international firms created by the devolution of their consulting divisions by the major accountancy firms some years ago.

MAXIMIZING THE VALUE DERIVED FROM EXTERNAL EXPERTS

An approach increasingly used by companies is to have external experts deliver a substantial body of work – an extensive cost reduction programme, say, leading to numerous contracts – and then keep the experts working afterwards on a part-time basis. There are a number of benefits of this approach, including:

- Cost-effectiveness for the company.
- Company staff will have access to an expert on an ongoing basis, and have their competences developed as a result.
- The expert is less likely to become 'stale'.
- Strategies are more likely to remain 'on track' over time, and contracts proficiently managed, delivering the expected benefits.

MATCHING BUYER PERSONALITIES/APTITUDES TO TASKS

Buying is much like any other profession – there are a striking number of people in it who shouldn't be. Square pegs in round holes, so to speak. I regularly come across buyers whose personalities and aptitudes are poorly matched to their buying responsibilities.

I freely admit to a personal aversion to buying chemicals and polymers, particularly where there are few vendors, and they can therefore all too often 'call the shots'. But there are individuals who have spent long and happy careers buying chemicals and polymers.

Most of the highest-performing buyers I know are people with high levels of intellectual curiosity, and they have a strong drive to understand why things are how they are – so they can develop options to change them. Such people tend to be fairly driven, they prefer managing risks to avoiding them, and some do not make very happy team members. They want to be held accountable for their own actions, not others' actions, and to be judged and rewarded accordingly.

BUYER MOTIVATION AND INCENTIVIZATION

As you might expect, buyers differ greatly from one another in what they find motivating. I have met buyers who are perfectly honest about being principally motivated by money. Such people seek positions where they can save a great deal of money for their employer, and personally benefit handsomely as a result. But I've also met many buyers who seem quite unconcerned about their income, and will happily save their employer millions of pounds over the years, without having to be incentivized to do so.

INDIVIDUAL ROLES, RESPONSIBILITIES AND AUTHORITIES

This is a much neglected, but important area. It is central to the success of cost reduction programmes that the buyer is totally confident about the flow of information between their company and the potential vendors. It follows that they must have confidence in any colleague(s) who communicate with potential vendors, that they will not compromise the buyer's position.

The rationale for being very clear about individual colleagues' roles, responsibilities and authorities emerges from the buying cycle (Chapter 3). Vendors – both current and potential – will seek to influence some of the cycle stages, with a view to increasing their prospect of being awarded the coming contract, and on better terms than might otherwise be the case.

To illustrate the point, let's take a scenario where two capital equipment manufacturers are seeking to supply their own design of an item of capital equipment to the buyer's company. The buyer's colleagues are quite unconcerned about the final choice of vendor, on quality and other grounds. Let's say one vendor, through the tender process, quotes a price of £900,000, while the second vendor quotes a price of £800,000. Now if you inform your colleagues about the quotes, but you haven't made it perfectly clear that they are not to communicate with the vendors, a colleague might unwittingly inform the second vendor (whether overtly or subtly) that their bid is the most competitive, and they can expect to hear some good news soon.

But if we assume there has been no collaboration between the two vendors, and the tender process has been executed proficiently, the quotes will have been the vendors' first bids. Who is to know how much further they might have been prepared to drop their prices? One thing is for sure – the second vendor will not drop their prices, once they learn that their bid is the lowest on offer to your company.

There are numerous other ways in which vendors can – and do – compromise the buying cycle. For such reasons, it has long been my policy to share confidential information – such as quotations – with colleagues on a 'need to know' basis. I can be accused of not being a good 'team player', and the policy does often cause resentment, but neither matter bothers me in the slightest. And the policy has undoubtedly helped me save millions of pounds more for my employers and clients over the years than if I were more interested in keeping colleagues 'in the loop' with no good justification.

BUYERS' PRODUCT KNOWLEDGE

There are a few spend areas where intimate product knowledge is vital to success, and the fields of food and clothing are often cited. I often comes across buyers who attribute their 'success' in a particular spend area to their lengthy experience. But almost without exception, with such people, I find I am able to make significant improvements to the prices they're paying. I may or may not be more intelligent than them, but what I can bring to the party is a fresh eye. I can review the area dispassionately, not having the 'baggage' of lengthy exposure to the market.

BUYERS' CONTRACT LAW KNOWLEDGE

When I started my career as a professional buyer in the 1980s, it was generally held essential for buyers to have a strong grasp of contract law, and to be able to develop and negotiate complex contract terms. Many people still hold this to be true, but others are of the view that in-house or external legal expertise might perform a useful supporting role, to the point that buyers' legal expertise need not be at a high level.

BUYERS' COMPETENCE DEVELOPMENT

In my view, the best way for buyers to develop their competence over time is to work on a variety of spend areas – both goods and services – for a variety of employers, in a variety of sectors, and include some years working for a specialist procurement consultancy. This width and breadth of experience will help them make the 'mental connections' that will enable them to deliver consistently strong results.

To give a personal example of such 'mental connections', in the 1990s I started working for the UK division of a major logistics company. Within my 'portfolio' was mechanical handling equipment (MHE), capital equipment such as forklift trucks. A case study on the area appears in Chapter 4. Now I had no technical knowledge of such equipment, but it happened that I had previous experience of buying and managing large 'fleets' of photocopiers, and I realized that there were some interesting parallels. That is, in both cases, the buyer's company wants high equipment reliability, and to manage the assets, for example by circulating equipment around the company to better match assets with workloads. The result of my 'mental connection' was £500,000 pa savings for my employer.

There are a number of organizations in the UK offering courses in various procurement-related areas, including CIPS. Recent course offerings from CIPS are outlined in Appendix 3.

PERFORMANCE MEASUREMENT AND REPORTING

There are numerous issues around which the performance of procurement functions and executives might be measured, but given this book's focus on cost reduction, I shall focus on this area here.

In Chapter 1, I wrote of my admiration for the buying philosophy outlined in a book (Sheridan, 1991), and the author also had typically robust advice to offer with respect to performance measurement and reporting. The rest of this section is drawn from the book.

There are perhaps two golden rules as regards producing the report on Purchasing's negotiating performance: be ruthlessly honest, and keep the methods of measurement essentially simple. It needs to be remembered that the purpose of measurement is twofold.

First, each function, each operating point within it, and each individual, needs to be motivated by agreeing achievable targets. Without targets, the essential element of competitive endeavour is likely to be lost... Because its (Purchasing's) nature is, or should be, so money oriented, its success or failure should be measured in similar vein. Although there will be some exceptions, measurements failing to reflect 'gains' in terms of monetary savings will contradict the raison d'être of the function, and tend to dilute its activity. Nothing should be allowed to detract from the function's main purpose.

Second, the functional performance achieved, when publicized, will be a projection of the expertise of the department and individuals within it, as perceived by both the board, and the heads of other disciplines...

There is never any point in living in a fool's paradise, nor in producing results that perpetuate that illusion, as far as others are concerned. Honesty of purpose demands that only improvements as a clear result of Purchasing's input should be claimed. It may sometimes prove tempting to report 'savings' that others might reasonably construe as 'stretching things a bit far'. If so, the 'saving' should be foregone or, at best, be included in a section separate from the main report, with an appropriate rider attached. If purchasing is to 'put itself on the map', then all external cynicism as to its capabilities must be eliminated....

In addition, complicated measurement methods tend to produce cynicism, not remove it. A claim supported by a host of riders and 'ifs and buts' is unlikely to convince a busy board that they have within their midst a dynamic, clear-thinking, entrepreneurial department capable of establishing detailed, unambiguous deals....

Measurements against 'standard costings' seem wholly unsatisfactory, despite the fact that this practice is widely followed in many organizations. The process usually consists of purchasing providing advance details to the cost accountants of anticipated prices of main supply items, enabling budget-holders to present their future plans to the board. In the case of revenue items, the projected prices, after some discussion between purchasing, accountant and budget-holder, will find their way into the cost of production and subsequently into selling prices.

Thus, Purchasing has a vested interest in projecting what might be considered by others (even if we allow for the complete honesty of purchasing management itself) as prices and terms higher than those believed to be actually achievable by little, or no, effort when the time arrives for negotiation...

If the measurement method is to be honest and effective, it is as well to know what NOT to include. Functional integrity and credibility are at stake, and set the relationship between department and board as well as other functional heads. The following represent the main areas where claims to negotiated benefits would best be foregone, if functional alienation is to be avoided:

- reductions in specification which clearly in themselves would be expected to result in lower prices, and which are the outcome of the end-user's own decision to change quality, or move to new technology;
- volume increases of such a degree, that prices could be expected to fall because of them;
- money market rate changes that produce automatic improvements in existing settlement terms, or credit facilities, without any action by the negotiator;
- notional 'gains' made by the refusal to accept a proposed price increase, or by reducing the size of that proposed increase;
- price reductions made voluntarily by vendors, without any input from Purchasing;

- reductions in prices caused as a result of a downturn in commodity prices quoted on world commodity-market exchanges – copper, tea, coffee, cocoa, lead, barley, wheat etc – and generally beyond Purchasing's control;
- price reductions made as a result of standardizations NOT introduced by Purchasing's initiative, or which failed to reflect any real coordinating role played by purchasing;
- capital items where no previous price comparison is possible, because the product has not been acquired before, or in the same form, and revenue items newly required, incapable of reasonably direct comparison with a previous product.

In times of galloping inflation (in the mid-1970s, retail price inflation reached almost 27 per cent in the UK), some allowance needs to be made in measurement terms, if even the most successful negotiator is not to be deprived of all plaudits. A demotivating target is worse than no target at all, and who can tolerate for long reporting nothing but failure if the mechanism is unrealistic?

But if inflation rates are moderate, say 4 per cent or so, then the principle should be that top negotiators will be more likely to stave off such effects on prices, to a far better extent than average or poor negotiators, working on the sure principle that what a vendor cannot extract from one buyer, will surely be recovered twofold from another.

ETHICS

To my mind, high ethical standards are the cornerstone of robust commercial relationships. If I had the power, I should make the offer of gifts or hospitality to buyers in the public and private sectors, and their acceptance by buyers, illegal acts. But until and unless that happy day dawns, I refer you to CIPS's Professional Code of Ethics, at the end of Appendix 3.

Appendix 1

Service level agreement (SLA)

This document is an SLA negotiated with a major print management vendor in the UK. It is available for downloading, at www.lpsconsulting.co.uk.

1. DOCUMENT HISTORY

Issue	Version Date	Description of change
1	18.9.06	Initial Document

2. INTRODUCTION

2.1 Background

2.1.1. The Customer has nominated The Supplier as its preferred print supplier. The Supplier will work closely with authorized personnel to develop and maintain an effective print procurement process. The Supplier should take full ownership of the Agreement, displaying a confident

proactive and innovative process, to reduce the wastage and administration burden associated with print procurement and management.

2.2 Purpose

2.2.1 The purpose of this document is to provide operational guidelines,
outlining the Service Levels that The Supplier and The Customer have
agreed to ensure that high standards are consistently met, and enhanced
through a policy of continuous improvement.

2.3 Scope

2.3.1 The areas covered by this Service Level Agreement are:
- Service levels – one-off print items, print stock items, packaging/
  labelling/delivery and service measures, customer service and support,
  staff availability and responsiveness, invoices, management information, competitiveness, conformance, value added and proactive
  management, management of change in style/format/re-branding.
- Management reviews.
- Key performance indicators.

2.4 Terms of reference

2.4.1 It should be noted that this document attempts to regulate the operational interfaces between the two companies, and this Service Level
Agreement (and all matters herein dealt with) is for the purposes of
ensuring correct standards are maintained to The Customer's satisfaction.
2.4.2 Any corrective actions raised as a result of a deficiency of this
Framework Agreement will not be treated as a current 'Customer
Complaint'. Both The Customer and The Supplier agree to:
- (A) Provide sufficient access and facilities to allow nominated representatives from either Company to audit the Agreement;
- (B) Nominate an Authorized Representative, who will act as the focal
  point for escalating corrective actions and quality issues. The
  identity of the Authorized Representatives may change over the
  course of the contract.

2.5 Process

2.5.1 The Supplier will provide The Customer with print management
services for any print related items required from time to time, but for
the avoidance of doubt this is not a sole supply agreement. This will be
achieved by utilizing The Supplier's facilities, specialist trade factories,
warehousing, and management facilities.

The location of The Supplier's storage site is:

The Supplier
<address>
<telephone number>

The location of The Supplier's production site is:
The Supplier
<address>
<telephone number>

3. SERVICE LEVELS

3.1 One-off Print Items
One-off print items are specialized printed items that are for a particular purpose, and are unlikely to be reprinted or held in stock.
3.1.1 Aim
(A) To liaise on an ad hoc basis with all parties concerned offering advice, costing and supply of any bespoke print requirements.
3.1.2 Approach to task
(A) The Supplier will advise on The Customer's bespoke requirements, offering a complete range of print and print-related manufacturing options.
(B) Each request will be fully quoted with consideration to budget and lead-time.
(C) The Supplier will liaise with authorized personnel on all aspects of design and artwork.
(D) The Supplier must be in receipt of a fully authorized purchase order from authorized personnel before any work can commence, unless exceptional requirements and time pressures make this unworkable.
(E) When requested, a proof will be provided to the authorized personnel. This will be in accordance with the lead-time set in the Order. Once approved, at least one signed-off copy should be returned to The Supplier.
(F) Once agreed The Supplier will oversee the production, ensuring the request is fulfilled to the standards set, and production method agreed.
3.1.3 Quotations
(A) Within twenty-four (24) hours of receipt of The Customer quotation request, The Supplier will supply quotations, and within twenty-four (24) hours of receipt of an Order, The Supplier will respond as to whether it can comply with the Order, and with confirmation of the price.

3.1.4 Lead Times and Delivery Dates

(A) Lead Times/Delivery Dates for one-off print requests will be agreed at the quotation stage, and unless The Supplier states otherwise at the quotation stage, the Delivery Date stated in the Order will be met.

(B) The Supplier will advise of any revised schedule, should the authorized person not be able to provide artwork, purchase order, or proof agreement as detailed at the outset.

(C) The Supplier will advise a revised Lead Time/Delivery Date should there be a change in specification, or quantity required.

3.2 Print Stock Items

3.2.1 Aim

(A) To manage the ordering, supply and stock control of all print that is held in stock, within the parameters set out and agreed by The Customer.

3.2.2 Approach to task

(A) The Supplier will receive orders by fax, e-mail, telephone or face-to-face.

(B) The Supplier will ensure all orders provide the necessary cost centre, where applicable. In addition to this, The Supplier will ensure correct authorization/approval has been gained for all requests.

(C) All queries will be raised within twenty-four (24) hours of receipt of order with the appropriate authorized personnel. The Supplier will advise on all matters relating to the product range, product codes, unit of measure and unit cost.

(D) For any new items requested, The Supplier will collate all relevant information from the authorized personnel, and agree stock holding and reporting requirements. This should be carried out within forty-eight (48) hours of the request.

(E) The Supplier will be responsible for ensuring stock levels are held at a level in keeping with recent product history, to maintain available stock for next day delivery. Stock levels will be agreed at the time of ordering, and will generally reflect a three (3) month usage, thereby reducing liability for redundant items, in the event of a re-branding/re-launch exercise.

(F) Stock will be financed by The Supplier and invoiced only upon delivery, or if the stock becomes redundant (only stock that has been previously agreed either by Order or an agreed stock level). The Customer will not be liable for any stock held that is over the three (3) month period.

(G) The Supplier will be responsible for ensuring that all stock conforms with the corporate guidelines set and agreed by The Customer.

3.2.3 Lead Times

(A) For all stock requests received before 16:00 hours, Monday to Friday, delivery will be made on the following working day.

3.3 Packaging, Labelling, Delivery and Service Measures

3.3.1 Packaging and Labelling

(A) The Supplier will ensure all goods are packed securely, to ensure that with all reasonable handling, the product arrives in good order at the point of delivery.

(B) The product will be consistently packed, observing correct units of measure.

(C) Each package will be clearly labelled with:
- Product Description
- Product number
- Delivery Location
- Requisitioner
- Quantity

3.3.2 Delivery

(A) The Supplier will deliver consignments within the hours of 09:00 and 17:30 unless by prior agreement. The delivery address will be indicated on the order.

(B) Each request will be supported by a delivery note detailing
- Product Description
- Product number
- Delivery Location
- Requisitioner
- Quantity

(C) Once the delivery is complete, proof of delivery details should be sent through to the authorized person. Hard copy should be archived for future reference.

3.3.3 Service Measures

(A) Appropriate records will be maintained for monitoring performance and compensation. The Parties agree that all compensation will be in the form of service credits.

(B) All deliveries of Goods will be deemed Business Critical. Failure to deliver by the agreed Delivery Date will result in an automatic fifty per cent (50%) reduction from the cost of the relevant Order. If The Supplier fails to deliver within twenty-four (24) hours after the agreed Delivery Date, The Customer will be entitled to a one hundred per cent (100%) reduction from the cost of the relevant Order.

(C) The parties acknowledge and agree that such reductions are a genuine pre-estimate of the Customer's loss in the event of delay.

(D) If The Supplier fails to deliver any Goods by the agreed Delivery Date on three or more consecutive occasions, The Customer will be entitled to treat such failure as a material breach of the relevant Order (incapable of remedy) for the purposes of the Framework Agreement.

3.4 Customer Service and Support

3.4.1 Aim

(A) To provide professional support to The Customer's authorized personnel, demonstrating the required expertise in all print areas.

3.4.2 Approach to task

(A) The Supplier will provide on-site customer support Monday to Friday (excluding statutory holidays) between the hours of 09:00 and 17:30.

(B) The Supplier will provide customer support by phone from the main manufacturing unit twenty-four (24) hours per day (excluding Christmas Day).

(C) All staff will have an advanced level of knowledge of The Customer contract requirements and corporate guidelines, and be able to offer advice whenever necessary.

(D) All staff will be fully conversant with all techniques and practices employed in the various stages of print and print production. This will extend to a complete understanding of the stock held, product codes, and requirements of The Customer authorized personnel.

3.4.3 The Supplier customer support team will:

(A) Strive to build a close working relationship with The Customer's authorized personnel, thereby developing an understanding of their specific needs.

(B) Liaise with The Customer's authorized personnel to ensure all orders are complete, and provide all the relevant details to allow accurate and effective recharging of the services.

(C) Be responsible for advising and managing all stages of the print production, from conception through to delivery.

(D) Give detailed feedback on the contract to authorized personnel at regular review meetings. This will provide the ideal forum for discussing any improvements that can be made to the service offered to The Customer.

3.4.4 Staff availability and responsiveness

(A) The Supplier must attend The Customer's London site within four (4) working hours of a request to assist with complicated quotations.

(B) The Supplier must respond within two (2) working hours for any aspect of customer service.

3.5 Invoices

3.5.1 Aim

(A) To provide timely and accurate invoices.

3.5.2 Approach to task

(A) A monthly invoice will be presented to The Customer within fourteen (14) working days of the end of the month.

(B) The invoices will provide the following information:
- Product description and quantity produced
- Quantity issued
- Purchase order number
- Details of Authorized Personnel

(C) The Supplier will ensure all Authorized Personnel are on The Customer's authorized list.

(D) All hard copy confirmation orders and delivery notes will be kept with The Supplier, and presented if and when required.

3.6 Management Information

3.6.1 Aim

To provide an accurate report on the monthly activity of the contract, detailing the overall performance, and any statistical changes that may lead to future cost considerations. Based on information provided, The Supplier will advise The Customer of any cost saving or performance enhancing initiatives that may be implemented.

3.6.2 Approach to task

(A) The Supplier will capture all relevant data throughout the month to allow accurate recharging of cost. This will be in a format agreed with The Customer.

(B) The Supplier will produce two reports on a monthly basis as follows: (i) a report concerning work-in-progress (WIP) and (ii) a report concerning completed work.

(C) The Supplier will provide monthly billings, five (5) working days after the month end.

(D) The Supplier will provide usage reports on any items stored on behalf of The Customer. These will highlight monthly trends, increased/decreased usage.

(E) The Supplier will advise on any cost saving opportunities that may arise.

(F) The Supplier will monitor slow moving stock items and report accordingly. If an item becomes redundant, The Supplier will provide details of stock held, and any cost implications to The Customer.

(G) The Supplier will provide a concise performance report indicating the success rate against the contract SLA.

(H) Should The Customer require further reports, The Supplier will where possible accommodate the request.

3.7 Competitiveness
3.7.1 Aim
(A) To maintain market competitiveness for all areas of print procurement and related items, in accordance with the terms and requirements of the contract or individual requests.
3.7.2 Approach to task
(A) The Supplier will monitor the market price to ensure all sub-contractors used in connection with The Customer contract clearly demonstrate they provide a value for money service.
(B) The Supplier will advise on any new manufacturing and/or distribution techniques, and their capabilities to meet the demands of the Customer contract. This will be substantiated by providing costing and sample products.
(C) Aided by reports produced detailing product activity, The Supplier and The Customer will review on a 6 (six) monthly basis, the cost of producing a set basket of products. Any deviance will be addressed in accordance with the contract.

3.8 Conformance
3.8.1 Aim
(A) To ensure that all printed items conform to The Customer's current agreed corporate guidelines.
3.8.2 Approach to task
(A) All requests for new/amended items should follow the correct authorization procedure, and be approved in the first instance by the Customer's authorized person for that area.
3.8.3 The Supplier will be responsible for quality assurance activities relating to the inspection of all items produced.
3.8.4 The Supplier will supply and keep updated a print 'reference book' covering all printed items.

3.9 Value Added and Proactive Management
3.9.1 Aim
(A) To provide a value added and proactive management style, to assist The Customer with their print procurement activities.
3.9.2 Approach to task
(A) To have regular formal and informal meetings with the print procurement team, so that The Supplier keeps authorized personnel up to date with changes in the print market.

(B) By providing the services outlined in this document, The Supplier will bring added value and a proactive management style to the print procurement activities.

3.10 Management of Change in style/Format/Re-branding
3.10.1 Aim
(A) The Supplier will liaise closely with the authorized personnel and be actively involved in the management of any print changes within The Customer.
3.10.2 Approach to task
(A) By regular formal and informal meetings with authorized personnel, The Supplier will keep up-to-date with changes within The Customer.

4. MANAGEMENT REVIEWS

4.1 There will be a minimum of four monthly meetings following the Commencement Date, and thereafter four formal quarterly reviews per annum of this SLA.

4.2 The review should as a minimum consist of the following:
4.2.1 Review of the performance statistics relating to each of the Orders under the Framework Agreement
4.2.2 Review of the SLA responsibilities and measurement methods

Simple and Transparent Performance Measurement and Fee Adjustment

The Supplier's SLA/fee adjustment measurement is based on a simple and transparent scoring profile, where The Supplier is penalized a point for non-compliance. This is captured and recorded online at the end of every project.

The SLA will be formally monitored at the monthly Customer management meeting to review penalties incurred. At this stage The Supplier and the Customer will discuss the reason that led to the penalty, where the client then adjudicates if this issue warrants a penalty point. The penalty points are then calculated and reconciled against the below scoring matrix. The percentage calculation is then offset against the 4% management fee for all invoices that have a point attributed.

Non-compliance points in month	Deduction of fees for the month
0–10	Nil
11–20	–1.25%
21–30	–1.75%
31–40	–2.25%
41–50	–2.75%
51–60	–3.25%
61–70	–3.75%
71–80	–4.25%
> 81	Review contract

KEY PERFORMANCE INDICATORS (KPIs) FOR MEASURING THE SUPPLIER'S OPERATIONAL PERFORMANCE

The following KPIs will be hard-coded into The Supplier's e-procurement tool:

Issue/measure	KPI requirement
Quote receipt: % of quotes received within agreed timelines	100%
Final quote timeliness: % of quotes received within two working days of receipt of the final specifications from agency or client	100%
Final quote receipt: % of projects/jobs conducted after a final quote	100%
Order confirmation receipt: % of jobs started with order confirmation	100%
Error free delivery: % of projects delivered error free	100%
Operational delivery: % of deliveries in full, on time, in specification (DIFOTIS)	100%
Management information timeliness and accuracy	100%
File copies: % of projects/jobs where file copies received	100%
Invoice accuracy and timeliness	100%
Brand guidelines: % of jobs produced within brand guidelines	100%

PARAMETERS TO BE MEASURED FOR THE PURPOSE OF IMPROVING OPERATIONAL PERFORMANCE

Correctly requested templates	How many requests for quotes were issued by The Customer or their agencies? – percentage who did not complete template correctly? (This will help The Supplier identify training requirements among Customer staff)
Amended final quotes	How many final quotes were amended by The Customer? – Cost impact? – Reasons why? – How many final quotes did The Supplier amend? – Cost impact? – Reasons why?
Live jobs	percentage of live jobs that changed (reasons why?)
Involvement	percentage of projects where The Supplier was involved from the beginning? Early involvement will help The Supplier improve unit cost and quality
Confirmation/Go-ahead	percentage of projects where The Customer provided online go-ahead within 48 hours?

Appendix 2

Template for a request for proposal (RFP) for the supply of goods and/or services

I use this document as the basis for my RFPs. It is available for downloading, at www.lpsconsulting.co.uk.

Key

Text in italics is guidance for buyers, and must be deleted before finally issuing the RFP.

<Text within arrows is to be used, modified or deleted by buyers.>
REQUEST FOR PROPOSAL (RFP)
FOR THE SUPPLY OF
<NAME OF GOODS AND/OR SERVICES>
TO <COMPANY NAME>

<DATE>

It is recommended that the RFP, and any associated documents, are e-mailed as attachments rather than posted to potential vendors, and in the body of the e-mail, state the need for the vendor to acknowledge (also by e-mail) safe receipt of your e-mail and attachments within two working days. This will save you time and provide proof of the timed delivery of the same materials to each potential vendor.

TABLE OF CONTENTS

1 BACKGROUND

1.1 Introduction

Provide outline information on the spend area(s), current demand levels and projections, current arrangements, reason for the RFP, objectives. Avoid including current spend in this area, as this would guide potential vendors to ruling price levels, when they might otherwise have been prepared to offer far more competitive pricing.

1.2 Company profile

<insert a brief company profile, to the extent necessary to help the vendor understand the context of the RFP. State your company's website address if appropriate.>

We seek mutually beneficial relationships with vendors of goods and services, operating through clear contractual Terms & Conditions.

1.3 Scope of this RFP

<Boundaries of this RFP, eg which offices or plants are included or excluded, which ancillary services are included or excluded.>

2 ISSUES SURROUNDING THE RFP PROCESS

2.1 Confidentiality

All communications between us and vendors are to be regarded as confidential, unless otherwise advised in writing by us. All communications from vendors will be treated by us, our employees and advisors, as confidential, and their circulation will be strictly controlled.

We reserve the right to immediately exclude any vendors found to be in breach of confidentiality, and to take any action we deem necessary in pursuit of remedy of such breach. In the event that any vendor is excluded on the grounds of a breach of confidentiality, we will require the immediate return of all materials supplied to the vendor in respect of this RFP, together with copies of any of these materials made by the vendor.

We recognize that vendors may wish to use third parties to assist in the preparation of their Proposal. Vendors are required to advise of the identity of these third parties, together with their role, prior to giving them any information relating to this RFP. We reserve the right, at our sole discretion, not to allow vendors to share information relating to this RFP with third parties.

Vendors are required to maintain a register of all employees and third parties, who have access to any information provided in confidence by us, in relation to this RFP. Vendors are further required to obtain from such employees and third parties, signed undertakings of confidentiality. Vendor must make both the register and the signed undertakings of confidentiality available for inspection by us if so requested.

2.2 Costs

Vendors are responsible for all their costs associated with their response to this RFP.

2.3 Instructions

Throughout this RFP there are a number of Instructions which vendors should regard as mandatory for the purposes of preparing their Proposal. These Instructions are identified by a heading:

Instruction x

where x is a unique reference number. All instructions must be complied with.

2.4 Intellectual property

All materials provided for the purpose of this RFP are, and will remain, our intellectual property.

No part of these materials may be reproduced, stored, or transmitted in any form, other than for the purposes of preparation of a Proposal, without our prior written permission.

We reserve the right, at our sole discretion, to immediately exclude any vendor found to be in breach of intellectual property rights, and to take any action we deem necessary in pursuit of remedy of such breach.

2.5 Questions and contact(s)

The purpose of the 'single point of contact' approach is to seek security and accuracy in information exchange between the vendors and ourselves. However, in the case of some complex spend areas, it might be preferable to divide the area between different managers eg manager x for technical issues, manager y for commercial issues, in which case the following sections should be modified accordingly.

During the period of this RFP, all contact with the firm in relation to the RFP must be through the designated contact(s):

Name: <insert>
Address: <insert>
E-mail: <insert>
Tel: <insert>
Mob: <insert>

Please note that your Proposal is not to be sent to the person(s) above, but to the individual named in Section 3.3.

Instruction 1

Vendors are required to confirm their understanding and acceptance of the above regarding:

- confidentiality
- costs
- instructions
- intellectual property
- questions and contact(s)

3 THE RFP PROCESS

3.1 Issue of RFP

This RFP and associated documents have been issued to potential vendors electronically on <dd/mm/yy>. The following timeframes are envisaged, but deadlines may drift at our sole discretion, in the event of unforeseen circumstances:

Stage	Deadline for stage completion
Vendor proposal receipt	<5pm dd/mm/yy>
Proposal evaluations	<5pm dd/mm/yy>
Notification to individual vendors of an intention to continue (or not) with detailed discussions/negotiations	<5pm dd/mm/yy>
Detailed discussions/negotiations	<5pm dd/mm/yy>
Decision on vendor(s) to be appointed	<5pm dd/mm/yy>
Notification to vendors of their appointment (or non-appointment)	<5pm dd/mm/yy>
Contract(s) start date(s)	<insert>

3.2 Questions

Following the release of the RFP, all vendors will be permitted to submit questions. These questions must be submitted by e-mail to the contact(s) named above in section 2.5. All questions must be reviewed, but we reserve the right to limit the format and content of responses. Where we respond to any question, the original question, together with the relevant response, will be sent to all vendors.

3.3 Delivery of Proposals

For contract values actually or potentially in excess of £x pa, or £y overall, or beyond z years' duration, in other words major commitments, it is recommended that Proposals be opened in line with the following procedure, to avoid potential accusations that all vendors were not treated equally at this stage. Each company plant/office will have at least one 'named individual' carrying out the role of opening Proposals in the presence of the named contact (section 2.5). The named individual will be responsible for (a) the safekeeping of one unopened Proposal from each vendor, (b) e-mailing the vendors authorizing them to send an electronic copy of the Proposal to the named contact.

<Two Proposals – or more if appropriate – must each be placed into a well-sealed envelope, and all envelopes placed within a well-sealed outer. The outer must be delivered to the individual named below, by a deadline of 5pm dd/mm/yy, clearly stating on a label on the front of the envelope, 'For the attention of <insert name>, response to RFP with regard to the supply of <name of goods or services>'. It is planned the responses will be opened within two working days of the deadline.>

All Proposals must be received before the above deadline; if received after that time they may, at our sole discretion, not be considered. In the very unlikely event that we accept a Proposal after the deadline, that Proposal will remain unopened until such time that all Proposals can be opened simultaneously.

The Proposals are to sent to <insert name, job title and address>.

The individual named above will contact you by e-mail after all Proposals have been opened, and authorize you to e-mail a copy of the key elements of your Proposal to the individual(s) named in section 2.5.

3.4 Proposal evaluations

We have prepared a set of evaluation criteria that will be used to assess all submitted Proposals.

<Criteria to be outlined. For most major projects they will include the following at the least:

- financial viability
- cost competitiveness
- capacity and capability
- anticipated 'fit' with our future anticipated requirements
- willingness to trade under our contractual terms
- duration and quality of our existing trading relationship, if any
- our assessment of the risks involved in awarding you our business, including potential disruption if moving from existing arrangements
- information received from reference clients>

3.5 Post-Proposal discussions & negotiations

The vendor(s) whose proposal(s) best meet our evaluation criteria, as outlined in section 3.4, shall be invited for detailed discussions with our staff, and any advisors deemed appropriate.

3.6 Notification of unsuccessful vendor(s)

We will offer a briefing to any unsuccessful vendor(s) who request one. We reserve the right to control the location, format, content and timing of any such briefing.

Instruction 2

Vendors are required to confirm their understanding and acceptance of the RFP process:

- issue of RFP
- questions
- delivery of Proposals
- Proposal evaluations
- Selection of vendor(s) for post-Proposal discussions & negotiations
- Post-Proposal discussions & negotiations
- Notification of unsuccessful vendor(s)

4 CONTENT AND FORMAT OF PROPOSALS

4.1 Content

Proposals must as a minimum contain a table of contents, documented responses to each Instruction, and documented responses to each requirement.

Proposals must be substantial enough to demonstrate that the vendor has understood, and is attempting to comply with, the relevant Instruction or requirement.

You may submit an innovative and/or non-compliant Proposal **as long as it is accompanied by a fully compliant Proposal**. Such Proposals must be submitted in the form of a clearly marked Appendix. We reserve the right to disqualify vendors who do not submit a compliant Proposal.

4.2 Assumptions

Please detail any assumptions you have made in completing your response.

4.3 Promotional materials

You should refrain from including or referencing promotional materials in the main body of your Proposal. Any promotional materials submitted may be included in an Appendix, provided that they are clearly marked as such.

4.4 Sequence

Your Proposal must use the sequence and numbering of the requirements section of this RFP in the 'response to requirements' section of your Proposal.

4.5 Copies

'For contract values…' (see section 3.3). Ensure that you seek enough copies of the Proposal, so you can supply a copy to each individual who needs to review it, plus one copy for the 'named individual' in Section 3.3 to retain (as appropriate).

<number> hard <copy/copies> of the main body and appendices of each Proposal must be supplied, in line with the directions in section 3.3.

4.6 Format

At least one copy of your Proposal (including Appendices) must be provided on A4 paper, printed on one side only, and held in a ring binder.

4.7 References

Instruction 3

Please provide the following details for three current customers, the nearer their requirements are to ours, the better:

- name
- job title
- company
- address
- e-mail address
- telephone numbers (fixed and mobile)

Please ensure the individuals have formally consented to act as references, and confirm whether you need us to inform you in advance of our intention to contact them.

4.8 Appendices

You may wish to include pre-existing documents to support your Proposal. These must be included in the Appendices section.

Instruction 4

Vendors are required to confirm their understanding of the format and content of Proposals:

- content
- assumptions

- promotional materials
- sequence
- copies
- format
- references
- appendices

5 VENDOR PROFILE

5.1 Capability, capacity, financial viability, quality management systems

Instruction 5

Please provide an overview of your business operations in terms of capacity, capability and turnover, and how they relate to our requirements. From which locations would you service our account?

If not already provided, please provide two hard copies of your latest filed Accounts, to include the past 3 years' Balance Sheets, and Profit & Loss Accounts.

Please outline your quality management system(s), and indicate whether your relevant operation(s) are accredited to ISO9001.

5.2 Conflict(s) of interest

Instruction 6

Please advise of any actual or potential conflict(s) of interest that might arise if you were awarded a contract.

6 REQUIREMENTS

6.1 Details of requirements/specification

Give the fullest possible description of requirements. Wherever possible, provide detailed numerical information rather than broad statements. For Goods, wherever possible include a detailed technical specification, along with tolerances eg for copier paper thickness, 104 microns ± 3 microns. For Services, wherever possible include a Service Level Agreement and associated Key Performance Indicators ('KPIs) eg 'the copier service engineer will arrive at our premises within 3 working hours of our request, for a minimum 95% of _requests, measured over a period of 3 calendar months'. Ensure the vendor can deliver Management Information showing success or failure against KPIs._

6.2 Costs

Describe in detail how you want costs to be submitted, and ensure the unit of measure is clearly stated eg £/000 or £/kg.

Where appropriate, create and e-mail an Excel spreadsheet for the vendors to complete, including the formulae for calculating overall costs. This will simplify the spreadsheet analysis, which will be required once costs have been received from vendors. Suspiciously large cost differences between vendors may reveal the possibility of a gap in vendors' understanding. Test the possibility while being aware that the difference may simply be attributable to a highly competitive offer.

6.3 Payment terms

Our standard payment terms are as stated in out Terms & Conditions.

6.4 Quality, service levels/problem resolution

6.4.1 Quality

We consider the quality of goods and services supplied to us to be very important. Please outline how you would propose to measure and report the quality of the <goods and / or services> you would supply.

6.4.2 Service hours

The following – or a modification – may or may not be relevant to particular services.

<Core office hours are Monday to Friday 09.00 – 17.00, excluding Public Holidays.>

The following may sometimes be required for certain goods or services, and if so, provide details:

<On some occasions individual offices may require work to be carried out outside of these hours.>

Instruction 7

Vendors are required to provide details and costs associated with working outside core office hours.

6.4.3 Problem resolution

Although no problems are anticipated, we would like you to outline your approach to dealing with any problems which may arise during the course of the contract.

Instruction 8

Please provide a summary of your approach to problem resolution.

6.5 Management information

It is important to receive the level of information required to manage the contract, at an appropriate frequency, and establish over time whether performance is meeting or falling below that required by the contract. Don't ask for a volume of management information that you won't have time to process.

We require <insert frequency – usually monthly or quarterly> reports on the overall performance of the contract, and on the individual <goods and/or services> delivered.

The following Instruction may be deleted in favour of a detailed description of the management information required, in which case ask for confirmation that the vendor is able and willing to supply it in terms of content, and in the required software eg Excel.

Instruction 9

Please provide examples of documentation that could be used to report performance, along with a suggested frequency, at no charge to us.

6.6 Contract terms

The attached contract terms will apply to this contract. If any terms are unacceptable to you, please outline your reasons, and where appropriate offer alternative terms. Please be aware that your willingness to comply with our terms will be one of the key criteria in our evaluation of your Proposal.

As a minimum use your company's standard terms and conditions, but in most cases, they will need to be modified to reflect the particular requirement.

Appendix 3

The Chartered Institute of Purchasing and Supply (CIPS)

> This appendix contains:
>
> - About CIPS.
> - Membership.
> - Training and events.
> - Professional Code of Ethics.

CIPS (www.cips.org) is the professional organization for buyers in the UK and beyond, while the equivalent in the United States is the Institute for Supply Management, the ISM (www.ism.ws). This Appendix is intended to give the reader a flavour of the activities of CIPS, most notably its training activities. CIPS's Professional Code of Ethics is at the end of this Appendix.

There are seven grades of CIPS membership, from Affiliate to Fellow. The **Affiliates** grade is designed for individuals who do not wish to become professionally qualified, but have a strong interest in purchasing and supply. There are no entry qualifications for Affiliate grade membership, and annual membership at the time of writing is £157.00.

The remainder of the information in this Appendix is extracted from CIPS's website, and their 2007–08 Training Portfolio.

ABOUT CIPS

CIPS exists to promote and develop high standards of professional skill, ability and integrity among all those engaged in purchasing and supply chain management.

We are the leading body representing the field of purchasing and supply chain management. Established in 1932, we have grown to become the central reference for industry best practice, and our Professional Code of Ethics is the standard around the world. In 1992 we were awarded a Royal Charter, in recognition of our status as a centre of excellence and support for the profession.

We are well positioned to effectively serve the interests of all involved in purchasing and supply chain management. Membership can make an enormous contribution to both public and private sector businesses, delivering a tangible return on investment.

Membership recognizes your professional status, and helps you to keep up to date with latest developments, through a comprehensive range of courses, conferences and publications.

Developing the 'art and science' of purchasing and supply

Developing the body of knowledge of the purchasing and supply management function underpins everything we do, and is fundamental to our long-term strategy. Our research programme helps to shape responses to tomorrow's challenges by supporting vital academic research. Along with our consultative work with some of the world's leading organizations, this intelligence enables us to visualize the future of leading edge practice.

Continuously improving the professional standards of practitioners

A key aspect of our remit is to promote and maintain high standards of professional skill, ability and integrity amongst all practitioners engaged in purchasing and supply management. We do this through our professional qualifications programme and associated membership standard, and by providing public access training programmes, and a comprehensive range of learning resources. Our members are bound by a Professional Code of Ethics, and are encouraged to make a lifelong commitment to their own professional development.

Promoting excellence in organizations

Helping organizations achieve and maintain the highest standards, throughout their purchasing and supply management operations, contributes significantly to their effectiveness. We support organizations in a number of ways, from educating and training their staff, to improving their performance through assessment and accreditation of their purchasing and supply methods, and sharing of best practice between peer groups.

Representing the interests and views of individuals within the profession

We represent the interests of the profession and the views of our members in many ways. Our special interest groups are designed to encourage members to share their views and knowledge with the wider community. We are also directly involved in shaping Government and European Commission policy on procurement; our consultative response process allows us to represent members' views at the highest level.

MEMBERSHIP

Training, advice, support and internationally recognized qualifications

Join CIPS and you will become part of our 42,000 strong network of professionally recognized and qualified members, including leading business people, professional managers and academics. This opens up a world of opportunities for you to fulfil your potential.

Develop your skills with our best practice updates, qualifications, training courses and seminars. Access our exclusive job opportunities and career advice. Plus, through our exclusive CIPS Premier benefits package, you can take advantage of our legal helpline, and privileges such as discounts on home, car and health insurance.

A range of membership grades to suit your needs perfectly

We offer seven different types of membership, to cater for a wide range of professional and educational requirements. When you apply to join, we will consider your requirements and your qualifications, skills and experience. This will allow us to recommend an entry membership grade which suits you perfectly.

TRAINING AND EVENTS

Grow your skills with our comprehensive choice of training courses and events. For too long, purchasing has been neglected by top management. That position is now changing, as compelling evidence emerges about the strategic and operational impact of purchasing as a lever for maximizing shareholder value.

Professionals have to be armed with a more sophisticated competence mix, in order to rise to the challenge and maximize their corporate value. This requires the development of a radically different skill profile.

We provide an extensive range of training to suit purchasing and supply professionals at all levels. Our programmes are geared towards helping you deliver real strategic and sustainable value to your organization.

We are the key provider of purchasing and supply management training in the UK. Our enviable position as the leader in purchasing and supply management training is maintained through a constant development programme, our links with academia and commerce, and the excellent quality of our programme leaders.

Venues are hotels in various locations, making them accessible wherever you live in the UK. All of our events and venues are tailored to your needs, taking into account any physical, sensory or other disabilities.

Practical training courses (2007–2008)

Our practical training is designed for individuals who are inexperienced or new to purchasing and supply. These courses provide a comprehensive introduction to purchasing and supply techniques, from core competencies to the development of advanced purchasing management skills. We deliver over 200 of these events every year, the duration of which varies between 1 and 5 days. Forthcoming Practical training courses:

Purchasing

- Introduction to Purchasing
- Improving your Buying Skills
- Introduction to Practical Buying
- Environmental Purchasing and Responsible Procurement

- Development of the Buyer
- Effective Expediting
- Managing Purchasing
- Supplier Appraisal
- International Buying
- Forecasting Techniques
- Performance Measurement
- Buying Services
- Risk Management in the Supply Chain
- Supply Chain Management

Negotiation

- Introduction to Negotiation
- Effective Purchasing Negotiation
- Practical Negotiation
- Adding Value with Creative Negotiation
- Advanced Negotiation Workshop

Finance

- Dissecting a Supplier's Cost Structure
- Business Finance – what buyers need to know
- Reducing your Overheads

Relationship Management

- Understanding Sales Techniques
- Managing People in Purchasing
- Commercial Relationships
- International Business Relationships

Influencing Skills

- Confident Behaviour in Relationship Management
- Presentation and Communication Skills
- Understanding NLP
- Leading and Influencing in Purchasing

Legal

- Basic Contract Law
- Commercial Law

- Legal Aspects of Purchasing
- Exploring and Developing Terms and Conditions

Contract Management

- Specification Writing
- Managing the Tendering Process
- Tender Analysis
- Introduction to Contract Management
- Effective Contract Management
- Improving Service Delivery
- Facilities Management

Stores Management

- Introduction to Storekeeping
- Inventory Management
- Stores Management

Seminars

CIPS also runs a number of seminars each year, the following being those run in the second half of 2007:

- Fundamentals of Buying Telecommunications
- Buying Business Travel
- The Procurement of Specialist Contract and Temporary Workers
- Buying Legal Services
- Buying Security Services
- Buying Corporate Wear – defining your brand and image
- Energy – Commodity Buying in a Volatile Environment
- The Fundamentals of Buying and Managing Consultants
- The Principles of Buying Distribution Services
- Buying Catering Services
- The Insider's Guide to Agencies
- An Introductory Seminar on Buying Advertising
- Understanding and Buying Design
- Understanding IT Procurement
- A Commercial Approach to Data Protection in Procurement
- A Commercial Approach to Software Agreements
- Purchasing Matters – Software Licensing
- IT Disputes – Clearing up the Mess

- A Commercial Approach to IP in Procurement
- Law for the Buyer
- Contract Drafting
- Making Contracts – the fundamental legal principles for buyers and suppliers
- EC Procurement Directives
- Successful Project Management
- Risk and Resilience in Food Supply Chains
- New Approaches to Measuring Purchasing Performance
- Procurement and the Internal Agenda

CIPS runs a number of 'Masterclasses' for senior procurement executives; the following were run in the second half of 2007:

- Revenue, Risk and Regulations
- Executive Decisions
- Management Consulting
- Executive Influencing Strategies
- Global Sourcing

In-company training programmes

Our in-company training offers innovative training solutions to help you realize the full potential of your purchasing and supply team. Whether you want to encompass the entire purchasing and supply process, or to tackle specific issues, we can create an in-company training solution that delivers a tangible return on investment for your business.

The training can be tailored to meet your specific needs, and can be conveniently delivered on your own premises. That means minimum disruption with maximum results, because candidates learn, literally, 'on the job'.

We are in the unique position of having the full resource of the Institute at our disposal. We can access a substantial knowledge and information pool, giving you the benefit of the latest thinking, research, networks and quality control. Our relationships with both academic institutions and leading specialists enable us to offer a wide base of expertise.

From short courses to long-term structured programmes, group sessions to individual director-level coaching, we have a proven track record across public, private and not-for-profit sectors.

Working in partnership – perfectly integrated with your strategy and operations

The key principle we adhere to is working in partnership with you to ensure total integration with your overall corporate strategy.

Our in-company training utilizes the very latest industry developments and resources and we have over 60 experienced specialist practitioners at our disposal, so we can provide exactly the right 'fit' for your organization.

Exemplary project management and on-going reviews come as standard, ensuring that agreed objectives are met at every stage of your training.

Training methods include:

- Diagnostic review and skills analysis
- Interactive tutoring
- 'Hands-on' application via existing organization projects
- Group discussion and seminars
- Role-playing
- Business games and team activities
- E-Learning

Range of topics

Choose from a wide range of topics. We work with you in the early stages of a training assignment, to identify the skills gaps within your organization, and formulate appropriate content. Your tailored programme could incorporate modules on any of the following topics:

- Purchasing strategy
- Commercial awareness
- Value chain improvement
- Managing business relationships
- Risk management
- Negotiation
- E-Procurement and process integration
- Managing cultural diversity
- Presentation skills
- IT in purchasing
- Contract law and management
- Influencing and persuading
- Retail buying

Bespoke training and professional qualifications

Combining bespoke training with our professional qualifications. We have the unique ability to combine professional qualifications with our in-company training programmes. This means that you can also work towards our accredited diplomas / certificates as you train in-house. We call this integrated approach the 'CIPS Corporate Award'.

The essence of the Corporate Award is that rather than studying in isolation on theoretical projects, you can immediately apply the knowledge you gain within the working environment. Instead you undertake work-based project – assignments, case studies and tuition are geared towards real data from 'live' organization projects, wherever possible. This means that the work you undertake is directly relevant to your business and capable of implementation, with the potential of delivering tangible return on the investment in training.

Our Corporate Award includes a full support service for each student on your team. We support you through your study, help to resolve problems and facilitate research.

The first level of our Corporate Award leads to a Corporate Award Procurement Certificate, and awards Associate Membership status. At the more advanced level, you can gain the Corporate Procurement Diploma, which confers full membership and permits you to use MCIPS after your name.

Studying for our Graduate Diploma can be a challenge, but many students find that they can obtain invaluable support from working with colleagues on an in-company programme. We can provide cost-effective, modular study programmes, with special examinations scheduled to suit your work patterns.

Conferences

Conferences encouraging collaboration, discussion and networking

Our conferences focus on a specific business issue or hot topic and analyse it from a variety of standpoints. Not only is purchasing and supply represented both from a presenter and delegate perspective, other relevant business disciplines will also be invited to take part. Both public and private sectors are represented, and all industries involved.

Generally, conferences will feature multiple speakers, offering a variety of presentation styles. The presence of delegates and speakers from both sides of the subject under discussion, helps to break down barriers, and enhance the practical outcomes of the event. The programme will range from plenary sessions, followed by discussion, to case studies and workshops where you can ask questions, contribute to discussions, share the challenges you face, and the solutions that you have developed.

Where appropriate, we will stage an exhibition alongside a conference, giving you the chance to meet vendors offering solutions that are relevant to the content of the event. Many of our conferences offer networking opportunities beyond just refreshment intervals, including social events the evening before, or an extended networking time once the business programme has come to a close.

Forthcoming conferences:

- 2nd Annual CIPS Middle East Conference – 'The Winning Agenda'
- Strategic Media Planning & Buying
- The Premier Conference: Risk and Reward in a Global Marketplace
- Marketing and Purchasing Conference...ensuring return on investment
- Efficient & sustainable public sector procurement

In-depth, interactive workshops for senior practitioners

Our workshops focus on one subject, and will usually be led by a single facilitator. The style of imparting knowledge is interactive, drilling down into the subject in more detail, with the emphasis on discussion. These events are particularly suited to the more advanced purchasing and supply practitioner, covering both practical and more strategic issues.

- The Principles of Buying Distribution Services
- A joint industry forum on production de-coupling
- Print Procurement
- IT Procurement in Action
- Fundamentals of Buying Telecommunications
- New Approaches to Measuring Purchasing Performance
- Buying and Managing Company Car Fleets
- Purchasing Matters – IT Disputes – clearing up the mess
- Leasing – realizing the savings
- Buying Digital and PR Services
- Buying Business Travel
- Understanding and Buying TV Production
- Procurement and the Internal Agenda: extending the sphere of influence
- Purchasing Matters – Software Licensing
- Buying Catering Services
- Buying Corporate Wear

- A Commercial Approach to Software Agreements
- Risk and Resilience in Food Supply Chains
- The Procurement of Specialist Contract & Temporary Workers
- A Commercial Approach to Intellectual Property in Procurement
- Buying Business Travel
- Law for the Buyer
- The Insiders Guide to Agencies
- Understanding IT Procurement
- EC Procurement Directives
- Purchasing Matters – A Commercial Approach to Data Protection in Procurement
- Buying Security Services
- Energy – Commodity Buying in a Volatile Environment
- The Fundamentals of Buying and Managing Consultants
- Successful Project Management – strategy, planning and implementation
- Contract Drafting

Masterclasses

Tailored masterclasses for business leaders

Our masterclasses are facilitated by experts from a range of backgrounds, with a vast and deep range of experience. The classes are discussion-led, and focus on a single subject, ranging from complex business strategy to personal development issues.

These one-day events are restricted to limited numbers, and are ideal for senior practitioners, whether engaged in procurement full-time or with responsibility for purchasing and supply as part of their role. Our lecturers are able to tailor the day as required, ensuring that your business gains maximum value from the event.

- Procurement Leadership Masterclass
- Strategic Procurement Execution Masterclass – how to make best practice ideas and strategies work
- Executive Influencing Strategies
- Global Sourcing – from strategy to implementation
- Revenue, Risk and Regulations
- Executive Decisions Masterclass – dilemmas, directions and destiny for procurement

Study and qualify

Reap the rewards of our comprehensive education programmes.

Our commitment to people development is central to our education programmes – ensuring that we offer a wide range of qualifications with supporting training programmes, materials, textbooks and networks.

We recognize the broader purchasing and supply processes perspective and also support the development and application of specialist expertise in different parts of the supply processes.

Training and development opportunities are available to applicants regardless of their location. There are currently over 20,000 members studying for our qualifications worldwide.

Our education programmes provide opportunities at several levels, to enable you to pursue studies in the context of your broader business environment.

CIPS' PROFESSIONAL CODE OF ETHICS

The following Code was approved by CIPS in October 1999.

Professional Code of Ethics

An introduction to our code of ethics

1. Members of our Institute undertake to work to exceed the expectations of the following Code, and will regard the Code as the basis of best conduct in the Purchasing and Supply profession.
2. Members should seek the commitment of their employer to the Code, and seek to achieve widespread acceptance of it among their fellow employees.
3. Members should raise any matter of concern of an ethical nature with their immediate supervisor or another senior colleague if appropriate, irrespective of whether it is explicitly addressed in the Code.

Key principles

4. Members should always seek to uphold and enhance the standing of the Purchasing and Supply profession, and will always act professionally and selflessly by:
   - Maintaining the highest possible standard of integrity in all business relationships, both inside and outside the organizations where they work.
   - Rejecting any business practice which might reasonably be deemed improper, and never use their authority for personal gain.
   - Enhancing the proficiency and stature of the profession, by acquiring and maintaining current technical knowledge, and the highest standards of ethical behaviour.
   - Fostering the highest possible standards of professional competence amongst those for whom they are responsible.
   - Optimizing the use of resources for which they are responsible, or influence, to provide the maximum benefit to their employing organization.
   - Complying both with the letter and spirit of:
     - the law of the country in which they practise.
     - Institute guidance on professional practice.
     - contractual obligations.

5. Members should never allow themselves to be deflected from these principles.

Guidance

6. In applying these principles, members should follow the guidance set out below:
    - Declaration of interest – any personal interest which may affect, or be seen by others to affect, a member's impartiality in any matter relevant to his or her duties, should be declared.
    - Confidentiality and accuracy of information – the confidentiality of information received in the course of duty should be respected, and should never be used for personal gain. Information given in the course of duty should be honest and clear.
    - Competition – the nature and length of contracts and business relationships can vary according to circumstances. These should always be constructed to ensure deliverables and benefits. Arrangements which might in the long term prevent the effective operation of fair competition should be avoided.
    - Business gifts – business gifts, other then items of very small intrinsic value such as business diaries or calendars, should not be accepted.
    - Hospitality – the recipient should not allow himself to be influenced, or be perceived by others to have been influenced, in making a business decision, as a consequence of accepting hospitality. The frequency and scale of hospitality accepted should be managed openly and with care, and should not be greater than the member's employer is able to reciprocate.

Decisions and advice

7. When it is not easy to decide between what is and is not acceptable, advice should be sought from the member's supervisor, another senior colleague, or the Institute as appropriate. Advice on any aspect of the Code is available from the Institute.

Appendix 4

Soft issues impacting on cost reduction drives

This appendix contains:

- Background.
- Corporate social responsibility.
- Sustainable procurement.

BACKGROUND

In recent years, there has been a marked increase in the extent to which commercial organizations are expected to respond to 'soft issues'. It is asserted that organizations – and larger organizations in particular, especially those 'in the public eye' – have far more responsibilities than merely creating wealth, providing employment and contributing taxes into the public purse. These 'deemed responsibilities' are many and varied, and some can impact on organization's buying activities, notably:

- environmental considerations, such as minimizing 'food miles', ie the distance that food is transported from the point of production, to the store;

- diversity issues, such as positive discrimination towards vendors owned by minority groups, or towards vendors who employ a high proportion of employees drawn from minority groups;
- Improving communities' well-being, in a number of ways;
- Improving the incomes of poorer farmers, most notably in developing countries, but also sometimes in the domestic market.

The extent to which you accept – or reject – the desirability of this wide 'remit of responsibilities' for organizations will largely depend on your political views, and this isn't a book about politics. But we do need to consider these issues with respect to cost reduction. In some cases, such as Sainsbury's supermarkets' buying of carrier bags (described in Appendix 5), it happens that the 'environmentally responsible' approach also saved the company money. But how should companies make a decision, when there is a conflict between these worthy objectives and the objective of minimizing costs? The guidance on this has to come from the top of the organization. In the absence of such guidance, there is a risk that individual buyers may pursue the 'soft agendas', often incurring additional costs for their company – possibly quite unknown to the company's owners.

CORPORATE SOCIAL RESPONSIBILITY (CSR)

CSR is 'a commitment to improve community well-being through discretionary business practices and contributions of corporate resources' (Kotler and Lee, 2005).

The nature of a company's public profile merits some discussion. A cynic might say that the less public a company's profile, the less the company needs to be concerned about 'soft issues'. But in some sectors, these issues are becoming ever more important over time. To illustrate the point, over recent years in the UK, for a variety of reasons, the activities of the major retailers have come under intense public scrutiny. And some of the major retailers are increasingly directing their offerings to that section of the public that is willing and able to pay a premium for goods and services, in return for an emotional return that they're 'doing good', with respect to matters such as the environment, farmer incomes in developing countries, and much more besides.

The resurgence of a number of iconic British retailers in recent years is at least partly attributable to their CSR programmes. A particularly interesting example is provided by Sainsbury's supermarkets, where they use the shorter term 'corporate responsibility'.

Corporate responsibility (CR) at Sainsbury's supermarkets

Sainsbury's 2007 CR Report, its fifth annual report in this area, is available on www.j-sainsbury.co.uk/files/reports/cr2007/files/report.pdf, and it's a model of clarity in this complex area. The Report states that five CR principles guide their activities, and Table A4.1 outlines the highlights in each area.

Table A4.1 Sainsbury's five corporate responsibility principles, and highlights of 2006–07

CR principle	Highlights of 2006–07
1. The best for food and health We work hard to make sure that we are meeting customer expectations and continually ask our customers what they think.	• Front-of-pack 'multiple traffic light' labelling on almost 4,000 products. • We were rated top for health by the National Consumer Council.
2. Sourcing with integrity Sourcing with integrity is about the way we do business, from the products we sell, to the way in which we procure them.	• We bought and sold to our customers 45 per cent of the entire British tomato crop. • Every single banana in our stores will be Fairtrade by July 2007.
3. Respect for our environment Climate change is a key driver for us so reducing energy, packaging and waste, are big priorities for our business.	• We are the first UK supermarket to offer customers a free carrier bag with a high proportion of recycled material. • We have committed to replace 150 million plastic trays and bags with compostable packaging on Sainsbury's ready meals and organic food by September 2008.
4. Making a positive difference to our community The supermarket sector is often reminded that its size and success should be harnessed as a public good. We agree.	• 31,000 schools are now registered for Active Kids. • £7.2 million raised for Comic Relief and £1.9 million raised for Sport Relief.
5. A great place to work We believe that supporting our colleagues in an inclusive environment, means treating everyone fairly.	• Proportion of female senior managers increased from 20 to 28 per cent. • Launch of the Colleague Wellbeing Charter.

SUSTAINABLE PROCUREMENT (SP)

SP is 'a package of actions to deliver the step change needed to ensure that supply chains... will be increasingly low carbon, low water and water efficient, respect biodiversity, and deliver wider sustainable development goals' (Her Majesty's Treasury, March 2007).

Interest in SP has largely been confined to the public sector in the UK, and a few high-profile large companies in the private sector. The interested reader is referred to the website of the Sustainable Procurement Task Force: www.sustainable-development.gov.uk/government/task-forces/procurement/index.htm.

For a commercial organization interested in pursuing SP objectives, some conflicts will need to be resolved between the 'soft' objectives, and cost reduction maximization – just as in the case with CSR.

Appendix 5

Buying at Sainsbury's supermarkets

Most manufacturers still have to learn what some of the large retailers grasped thirty or forty years ago: buying is as important as selling.

(*Peter Drucker*, Managing for Results, 1964)

This appendix contains:

- Overview.
- Goods and services for resale.
- Goods and services not for resale.

OVERVIEW

The first Sainsbury's store opened in London's Drury Lane in 1869, and over the intervening years Sainsbury's has become a British institution, its success 'based on a heritage of providing customers with healthy, safe, fresh and tasty food'. A few numbers from the company's latest annual report, covering the year to March 2007:

- annual sales £18.5 billion;
- excluding non-food sales, the company is the second largest grocery retailer in the UK, with around 15 per cent of the market (24 per cent in the London region);
- 490 supermarkets, 298 convenience stores around the UK;
- 16 million people visit a Sainsbury's store each week;
- operating costs reduction of £440 million across the period March 2005–March 2008 were on track.

But there's so much more to the company than would be obvious from the numbers. A visit to its website (www.j-sainsbury.co.uk) reveals a company with a very strong 'corporate personality', and it is highly active in a number of ways which appeal to its loyal customers – for example, its environmental initiatives, and support of Fairtrade suppliers. This is clearly a company that takes corporate responsibility very seriously. One small example is that the term 'staff' is rarely heard – executives talk about 'colleagues', whatever their seniority.

Following a period during which the company under-performed, Justin King (then 42) became chief executive in March 2004, following senior positions at Marks & Spencer and ASDA/Wal-Mart. A few months later, he unveiled a vision for the future, 'Make Sainsbury's Great Again' (MSGA). The initiative has been a great success, and progress is ahead of plan at the time of writing (November 2007).

Unlike some companies, retailers don't have an option about being proficient at buying. They wouldn't survive long if prices in their stores were significantly higher than the prices in their competitors' stores, regardless of environmental and other 'soft' considerations. So with the kind agreement of Justin King, I met with a couple of the company's senior executives, to discuss their approach to buying in general, and cost reduction in particular.

Retailers distinguish between two areas of buying: goods and services for resale (GFR) – the goods and services bought for resale to customers, ie the goods on display or promoted in stores; and goods and services not for resale (GNFR) – the goods and services bought to support the retailer's business activities, ie everything from commercial vehicles to carrier bags, advertising to electricity.

GOODS AND SERVICES FOR RESALE

I met with Amanda Heffer, one of the trading directors reporting to Mike Coupe, the overall trading director (Mike Coupe has sat on Sainsbury's

Executive Board since August 2007). The title 'trading director' may be unfamiliar to the reader, but in the retail sector it denotes a person with responsibility for buying the goods and services that are available for you to buy when you visit the store. In larger retailers, such as Sainsbury's, trading directors can have buying responsibilities for some billions of pounds every year.

Sainsbury's was understandably reluctant to divulge too much information about its highly regarded GFR buying team, but Heffer explained that there are six 'business units', each headed up by a director, such as Heffer, who is responsible for 'core grocery', ie groceries stocked at ambient temperature in the store. This business unit alone brings in £3.6 billion pa revenue for Sainsbury's.

Within each business unit there are between 3–7 categories, headed up by category managers. Category managers have a number of buyers reporting to them, along with a category planner, a range planner, and a number of category assistants. There is a close working relationship with specialists who work closely with the buyers, eg food technologists, concept developers, supply chain controllers etc – a significant cross-functional team.

I was struck by the frequency with which Heffer spoke of the importance of supplier relationships, well captured in her comment 'we work with suppliers for our customers' benefit'. Now she would hardly be in such a senior position without being very commercially astute, but she gave me a number of examples of where she and her team had worked in a cooperative manner with suppliers, to mutual benefit – particularly in terms of driving sales volumes, and delivering supply chain efficiency improvements, often through 'end-to-end reviews'. This philosophy was said to be prevalent throughout the company, and one of her colleagues provided a particularly interesting example of how Sainsbury's staff had worked with South African fruit growers.

CASE STUDY: SAINSBURY'S ANALYSES ONE OF ITS FRUIT SUPPLY CHAINS IMPROVES GROWERS' RETURNS, AND MAKES SIGNIFICANT SAVINGS ITSELF

Sainsbury's growers in certain southern hemisphere markets had informed the fruit buying team that their levels of financial return were not at the long-term sustainable level required to finance investment in new orchards and renew existing orchards.

The buying team approached the agents that worked on their behalf, and asked them for a full cost breakdown, so that all the costs in the chain – including the return to the grower – could be fully understood. In one of the southern hemisphere markets, there was a longer chain from the grower to the retailer, in that there was both a UK agent and a further agent at source.

The cost breakdowns gave Sainsbury's a very good understanding of the costs involved. In the end, Sainsbury's was able to give the growers a longer-term commitment, and by removing one of the agents it was able to improve the remaining agent's profitability, the growers' returns, and itself make significant savings. Now each price renegotiation is backed up with a real understanding of the agent's commission, and all the costs in the chain.

Sainsbury's is a keen believer in staff competence development, and distinguishes between 'leadership behaviours' and 'trading behaviours', the latter including commercial law and negotiation. Staff are required to have two formal reviews of their training needs every year, but informal feedback goes on all the time.

Sainsbury's is a keen user of e-procurement where appropriate (notably when rigid specifications are available), and has a small in-house team to manage the process for both GFR and GNFR spend areas.

The company takes advantage of 'grey market' opportunities, buying goods from countries at lower prices than it can obtain from the manufacturers' selling organizations in the UK. Recent examples have included coffee and washing-up powders.

The company also has 'global sourcing teams' in Poland and Hong Kong, respectively looking at sourcing opportunities in Eastern Europe and the Far East. Considerable efforts are made to ensure Sainsbury's fabled quality standards are not compromised.

Sainsbury's has a strict code through which it buys from suppliers, captured in a document also made available to the suppliers. The code covers the following areas:

- supplier selection;
- clear agreement at the outset of a trading relationship;
- fairness during the relationship;
- paying for promotions;
- third party involvement;
- spotting and solving problems;
- contract terms and conditions.

GOODS AND SERVICES NOT FOR RESALE

David Brooks, Sainsbury's head of revenue procurement, is responsible for over £1.0 billion pa of expenditure on GNFR, while a colleague is responsible for some £500 million pa on store construction and fit-outs (ie floors, shelving, refrigeration equipment etc). Both report into Neil Sachdev (commercial director), who recently joined Sainsbury's after 28 years with Tesco. Sachdev reports to Mike Coupe, Sainsbury's trading director.

Brooks currently has a team of 37 people, and is building the team up slowly, as Sainsbury's fortunes recover. His cost reduction target for the 2007–08 financial year is £40 million. He has five category managers reporting to him, each of whom manages a team of buyers, and there is also administrative support. Brief details of the team:

Category	Key spend areas	Level of stakeholder engagement	Buying staff
Supply chain	Third party logistics, haulage Commercial vehicles Agency labour	Moderate	4
Retail	Packaging, consumables Cleaning Security Catering Trolleys Waste disposal	High	9
Corporate services	Professional services inc. legal, consultancy, HR, Finance	Moderate	4
Customer	Advertising, print	High	4
IT	IT hardware and software	High	6
TOTALS			27

The buyers are supported by a team of 10 staff engaged in such activities as managing the e-procurement system, maintaining the contracts database etc.

In some spend areas, Brooks's team have a clear mandate to carry out their activities – 'a high level of stakeholder engagement'. But that's by no means the case for all spend areas. He was clear that he and his team have to win the 'hearts and minds' of colleagues in a number of departments, to become accepted – 'you have to be professional, you have to bring value'. But he has also put into place a mechanism to stop the proliferation of the vendor base (there are currently less than 3,000 GNFR vendors). No vendor can be added to the vendor base without Brooks's prior approval. And if they're not added to the vendor base, they won't get paid by Sainsbury's. It's a useful discipline.

Buyers are not heavily incentivized to meet cost reduction targets – 'that's what they're paid for', as Brooks explained. But buyers, category managers, and Brooks himself, are well rewarded when corporate targets are achieved.

Corporate targets relate to sales turnover, profitability and in-store goods availability to customers. I commented to Brooks that at – say – the buyer level, the individual would have a negligible part to play in sales turnover, and so would not be strongly motivated by the potential associated bonus in this area. And at this point, Sainsbury's strong corporate culture became very apparent. Brooks explained:

> We can all drive sales. Let me give you an example. A buyer has negotiated a maintenance contract with a vendor, to repair shopping trolleys. Now it's possible, for one of a number of reasons, that the vendor's performance is below that required by the contract. Too many shopping trolleys remain broken, and therefore not available for use by customers. If the buyer doesn't resolve the matter speedily and effectively, the result could be customers unable to find an operating trolley – which would reduce turnover, and leave a disgruntled customer. Not acceptable.

Brooks has tasked his team of buyers to engage with all the vendors within an 18-month timeframe. They are required to undertake at least one of the following activities:

- paper-based tender;
- e-enabled RFI or RFQ;
- e-auction;
- price benchmarking;
- face-to-face negotiations with incumbent vendors.

In common with many large organizations, Sainsbury's lays down clear guidance about how its buyers go about their duties. In the case of GNFR, this is contained within a 35-page 'Procurement Best Practice Guide'. The full details are confidential, but they include:

- different types of tendering, and how to execute them;
- different types of contracts;
- risk assessments;
- vendor appraisal;
- confidentiality agreements;
- portfolio analysis.

Brooks's team use the in-house e-auction capability around 50 times a year, and when I visited (October 2007) they had just run an e-auction for in-store promotional printed materials for the coming Christmas season, and achieved significant cost savings.

There are a few complex spend areas, where Sainsbury's relies on the expertise of independent companies to give it procurement guidance. Electricity is a good example, and it is obviously a large spend area for major retailers. Sainsbury's uses the services of Utilyx (www.utilyx.com) in this area, as do a number of other large UK retailers, including Tesco and Boots. Significant 'hedging' is carried out, to reduce the risk of highly volatile energy prices damaging the company's profitability.

One of Brooks's buyers, Beverley Whitfield, provided an interesting example of where she had worked closely with the company's carrier bags vendor to deliver environmental benefits and a cost reduction – a happy combination. The following case study concerns this initiative.

CASE STUDY: SAINSBURY'S DELIVERS ENVIRONMENTAL BENEFITS, AND ACHIEVES SIGNIFICANT COST SAVINGS ON ITS CARRIER BAGS

Major UK retailers buy their carrier bags from the Far East, where plastics and labour are less expensive than in the UK. Sainsbury's worked closely with its supplier of carrier bags and succeeded in reducing their impact on the environment (one of Sainsbury's five corporate responsibility targets), and modified the bag specification, without affecting the quality, or impact on customers.

The first element in the story was the bag specifications. First, the material specification was changed from 30 microns thick LDPE to 19 microns thick HDPE, and a third of the material was in-house factory waste. Then a small amount of very fine chalk was added, about 10 per cent of the bags' weight, to reduce Sainsbury's 'dependence on oil'.

The second element in the story was the packaging around the bags, to protect them during the journey from the Far East to the stores in the UK. The packaging had historically been cardboard boxes, but these posed a problem to the stores, because they could not be dropped off outside stores in inclement weather if the warehouse was full. The vendor changed the outer packaging and vacuum packed the bags, ie they extracted the air from them. This saved some 12 per cent of volume when transporting, giving both environmental and cost benefits. And the bags could be left outside stores in any weather conditions, and store staff would no longer have to dispose of cardboard boxes.

Sainsbury's is achieving significant cost savings, as a result of this environmentally friendly initiative.

Appendix 6

Buying at SmithKline Beecham

This appendix contains:

- Background.
- Structuring an effective cost management programme.
- Tactical control through purchasing category management.
- Buying at the right geographical level.
- Impacting total cost of acquisition.
- Determining appropriate category strategies.

BACKGROUND

You may be interested to gain some insights into cost reduction programmes in major international organizations. One well-documented story is that of SmithKline Beecham (SB), the firm which subsequently merged with Glaxo Wellcome to create GlaxoSmithKline (GSK).

SB's 'Simply Better Purchasing' programme in the early to mid-1990s was publicly credited with delivering cost savings of over £200 million. Elements of the story were outlined in an excellent book (Hughes, Ralf and Michels, 1998). Two of the co-authors, Jon Hughes and Bill Michels, were directors of ADR Consulting (www.adr-international.com), the procurement consultancy selected by SB as the change agent to support them, in the design and implementation of the programme. The third co-author, Mark Ralf, was senior vice president and group purchasing director at SB. The story that takes up the remainder of this chapter is drawn from the book, with the kind permission of the authors.

CASE STUDY: SMITHKLINE BEECHAM USES CASCADE TRAINING AND FUNCTIONAL CHANGE TO CAPTURE POST-MERGER SYNERGIES

When SmithKline French and the Beecham Group PLC merged in 1989, the resulting corporation, SmithKline Beecham, became one of the world's largest healthcare companies. With 50,000 employees selling 300 product lines, and laboratory services in 130 countries, SB had sales, at that time, of over £5 billion pa.

The cost of external purchases was over £3 billion pa, and represented 55 per cent of sales revenue. In 1990, however, purchasing was an undervalued function. There were no formal training and development programmes for staff. Little transfer of best practice was taking place. Staff were inadequately focused. Profit improvement was not yet on the agenda.

To change this, SB launched a three-year worldwide programme – Simply Better Purchasing – and targeted savings of £100 million. A cascade development programme was designed, to facilitate the required clarity of focus and boost functional competence.

1. A one-week launch conference was held for top purchasing directors worldwide;
2. Two phases of one-week-long training workshops were run for over 400 members of staff and 50 senior operations executives;
3. On-the-job coaching was facilitated by train-the-trainer workshops for 25 directors of purchasing.

Most importantly, the programme was geared not just for the full-time purchasing community, but for all staff with significant influence on sourcing and supplier management decision making. Attendees were drawn from marketing, research and development, clinical trials, technical and information resources departments.

Savings of £75 million in the first 18 months led to a doubling of the target to £200 million. This was achieved with ease.

Bill Michels, CEO of ADR North America LLC since 1996, worked on the programme, and recently reflected on it:

> It would be a mistake to gloss over the need for planned change, or the effort required to embed it. Anyone who has been involved in a major transformation programme will know that it cannot be achieved by simply overlaying a template onto an organization, ie by a third party simply 'doing something' to the client. It required a shared vision, together with an insightful change agent, and committed management.
>
> As a niche, knowledge-based procurement consultancy, we were selected as the change agent to support SB in the design and implementation of Simply Better Purchasing. Fresh from a highly successful four-year-long transformation programme with Reckitt & Colman (now Reckitt Benckiser), we designed a fit-for-purpose programme which spanned both production and non-production, and which comprised three phases over five years. Critically, the change was led from within, the business wasn't flooded with fresh faced MBA clad consultants, firing from their hips, wielding seven-step processes. The programme was moulded around the culture and structure of the business.
>
> During the early–mid-90s the content and concept of Simply Better Purchasing was visionary, and arguably set the benchmark for strategic procurement and category management (originally termed 'source planning'). Testament to this is that many of today's top procurement leaders 'came of age' through the initiative.

STRUCTURING AN EFFECTIVE COST MANAGEMENT PROGRAMME

When introducing planned purchase cost management, four sequential stages can usually be detected. They are illustrated graphically in Figure A6.1.

Initially, there is 'price drift'. This occurs when senior management have little real focus or grip on the supply chain. There are few cost controls. Price is determined by the market place. Inflationary price increases from vendors are common, and tactical skirmishing is the norm. Not surprisingly, relationships are invariably adversarial.

'Price down' marks the beginning of a true cost management campaign. It is about introducing straightforward tools to identify vendor strengths and weaknesses. In addition, tactical interventions

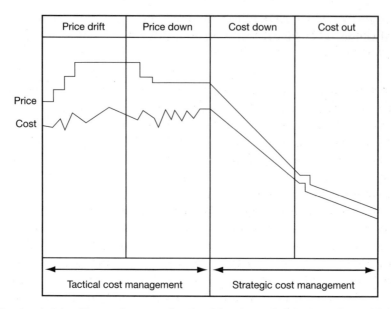

Figure A6.1   *Executives need to lead business initiatives that address both tactical and strategic cost management*

such as vendor reduction, negotiation and cost analysis, will achieve some reduction in vendor pricing.

'Cost down' and 'cost out' drives are radically different. They signal a business shift to more strategic cost management and the introduction of increasingly sophisticated margin analysis, capability development, vendor integration and profit-planning processes. The goal is to achieve fully transparent and jointly controlled buyer–vendor development programmes capable of taking cost out of the supply chain. Integrated with this is a similar drive to maximize value from vendors.

TACTICAL CONTROL THROUGH PURCHASING CATEGORY MANAGEMENT

Initially, many organizations are uncertain how best to move forward when launching a purchasing cost improvement programme. Clearly, this begins with senior management commitment. Bringing about permanent changes in cost structures will involve introducing new practices, challenging established procedures and creating more demanding expectations of what has to be achieved. This calls for 'champions of change' to sponsor the programme. It also calls for data.

A first step is to assess systematically the current focus on the full
buying portfolio. Identify the complete range of production and non-
production categories of expenditure that comprise total spend.
Figure A6.2 is a typical example to illustrate this.

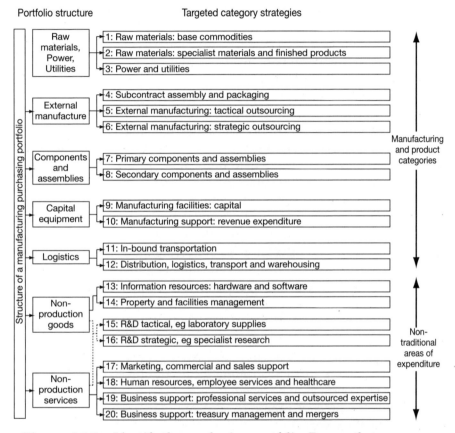

Figure A6.2   _Identify the purchasing portfolio. Ensure that you cover_
total spend. Then prioritize the cost reduction targets for attack

Now address the following questions, in a searching manner, with
regard to each of the categories:

- What recent analysis has been made of the expenditure on this
  category?
- Why is the product, good or service that comprises the category
  bought?

- What purchasing methods, tools and techniques are being applied?
- How does the expenditure on the category break down, in terms of individual business sites, and across specific vendors?
- Who are the 'influencers of sourcing', ie functional staff who are directly or indirectly involved with vendors?
- What criteria have been applied to vendor selection, and within what type of decision-making process?
- How has sourcing been managed over the past one to five years?
- What price trend data are available, and have cost drivers behind these prices been analysed?
- How long have current vendors been used?
- What is their performance, and how has that been measured?
- What in-company preferences, local ties, links and dependencies are there with specific vendors?
- To what extent are these helping or hindering the attainment of required business deliverables?
- What is the current status and nature of the relationship with each vendor?
- In what way should these relationships change?
- What is the record of vendors in delivering innovation, facilitating technology transfer, and supporting quality initiatives?
- What is the quality of management within prime vendors?
- What is their likely response to cost down initiatives?
- What potential sources of risk and vulnerability exist with core vendors? What plans are in place to reduce or remove them?
- What methods of contracting and payment are being employed? How effectively are these meeting the needs of both parties?
- When are contracts to be renegotiated?
- What is the preferred forward sourcing plan, over a period of not less than three years?

Challenging past thinking in this way is at the heart of buying category management. Cross-functional teams should be tasked with reviewing each of the major areas of expenditure, and producing forward sourcing plans. This process requires the generation of options, their systematic evaluation, and then the determination of an appropriate implementation plan. Senior management should demonstrate their determination to seek out new and radically different ways of moving forward. Pursuing such a route inevitably leads to major breakthrough change.

BUYING AT THE RIGHT GEOGRAPHICAL LEVEL

When challenging appropriate geographical positioning, it may be helpful to focus on a number of typical categories of expenditure. An example drawn from SB's European fast-moving consumer goods division is shown in Figure A6.3. It can be seen how a number of categories are positioned at the wrong level. Too much sourcing has been done at the local or country level, rather than at the regional level. Furthermore, global synergies with their US parent company were not being harnessed.

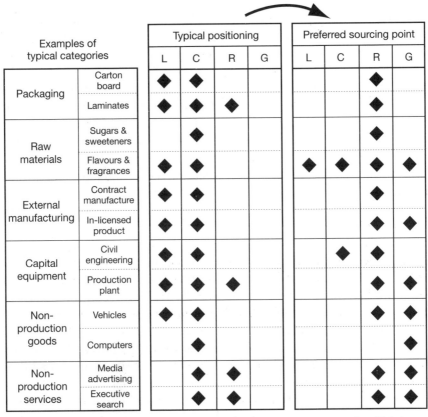

Examples of typical categories		Typical positioning				Preferred sourcing point			
		L	C	R	G	L	C	R	G
Packaging	Carton board	◆	◆					◆	
	Laminates	◆	◆	◆				◆	
Raw materials	Sugars & sweeteners		◆					◆	
	Flavours & fragrances	◆	◆			◆	◆	◆	◆
External manufacturing	Contract manufacture	◆	◆					◆	
	In-licensed product	◆	◆					◆	◆
Capital equipment	Civil engineering	◆	◆				◆	◆	
	Production plant	◆	◆	◆				◆	◆
Non-production goods	Vehicles	◆	◆					◆	◆
	Computers		◆						◆
Non-production services	Media advertising		◆	◆				◆	◆
	Executive search		◆	◆				◆	◆

L = Local   C = Country   R = Regional   G = Global

Figure A6.3   _Sourcing decisions should be taken at the highest possible geographical level to maximize leverage with suppliers_

When an organization decides to embark on this type of assessment, there are a number of questions that will need to be addressed:

- Is the internal supply organization operating at site rather than on a country, regional or global basis?
- How well is this internal structure functioning?
- What are the inefficiencies, expressed in financial terms, associated with the current approach?
- To what extent are vendors organized on a similar geographical basis, and where are customers located?
- Which vendors have sufficient capability, and commitment, to supply regionally and globally?
- Which organizational processes need to be strengthened, to ensure that knowledge and best practice can be successfully transferred from one country to another?

Balancing central control with decentralized collaboration enables a business to capture the benefits of centralization, while leaving the responsibility and authority for day-to-day management of local vendors with autonomous units. The challenge for executives is to work with their teams, and create a process for the active sharing of knowledge and the coordination of concerted actions across national and regional boundaries. By fully utilizing combined knowledge, total volumes and full bargaining power with vendors, substantial profit improvement can be achieved.

Introducing the approach usually leads to significant benefits for any business operating with decentralized operations, even when they are positioned across multiple market sectors. Furthermore, as well as reducing costs, the existing value delivery from vendors, such as quality, service, innovation, technology transfer and customer support, can be appreciably enhanced. In addition, there is a valuable but less tangible organizational benefit; collaboration improves the overall effectiveness of business operations, and strengthens team capability, right across the company.

In the early 1990s, pharmaceutical businesses were increasingly focused on managing their supply chains more effectively. Downward price pressures from governments and health maintenance organizations acted as the spur for change. The goal for pharmaceutical companies was to become low-cost producers.

SB was the benchmark standard in supply chain practice. A series of global initiatives were under way, designed to strengthen core capabilities, improve operating efficiencies and deliver superior value to customers. The deliverables were profitability, longer-term business competitiveness, and preferred customer status across the worldwide vendor network.

At the heart of SB's buying programme was category management. Eight programme elements were being pursued:

1. Attain managed control of all high-value-added bought categories of expenditure. Attack this £3 billion spend via six broad category families: raw materials; packaging components; external manufacturing; capital equipment; non-production goods; non-production services.
2. Standardize buying processes across countries. Significantly rationalize the vendor base.
3. Manage categories at the most appropriate geographical level. Adopt a migration plan: site to country, country to region, and region to global.
4. Create a highly competent buying resource. Ensure that sourcing strategies reflect defined linkages to business needs.
5. Accelerate significant improvement in cross-sector and cross-functional coordination.
6. Realign resources from transactional to higher-value-added activity.
7. Drive out complexity through business and vendor integration.
8. Prepare the supply base for future strategic business and manufacturing initiatives.

Cross-functional teams were tasked with reviewing each of the major areas of expenditure, and producing forward sourcing plans. This process required the generation of options, their systematic evaluation, and then the determination of an appropriate implementation plan. The key was a readiness to challenge the status quo, and for the business to be open to creative alternatives. Senior management demonstrated their determination to seek out new and radically different ways of moving forward. Pursuing this route led to major breakthrough changes.

IMPACTING TOTAL COST OF ACQUISITION

The task for both the buying organization and the vendor is to enhance the value delivered, by increasing the functionality of the product or service while reducing the total cost. This draws on value-analysis and value-engineering techniques to identify, and then eliminate or minimize, all non-value-adding processes and activities in the supply chain. The emphasis, therefore, is on the total acquisition cost of supply, and the value it brings to the end product. This requires the support and commitment of all functional disciplines within both the buyer's and the vendor's businesses. Using this approach, the aim is to:

- delete: eliminate non-value adding activities;
- reduce: minimize or eliminate usage;
- downgrade: ensure appropriate quality that is 'fit for function';
- substitute: identify and introduce alternative products or processes;
- replace: use something else;
- standardize: minimize or eliminate complexity;
- integrate: mesh in the processes and activities of production between the buyer and vendor.

DETERMINING APPROPRIATE CATEGORY STRATEGIES

Within the category planning process, it is important that team members consider the full range of potential options for cost reduction using the price down–cost down–cost out model. Furthermore, this will need to reflect the inherent complexity and centrality of the various categories of expenditure to any company's customer and product objectives. This is shown in Figure A6.4.

Consider the following sequence:

1. Segment expenditure by vendor, to determine those supply sources which can be controlled through open market competitive forces.
2. Introduce a robust vendor performance assessment process, to identify vendor strengths and weaknesses.
3. Rationalize the current supply base, through a comparative analysis of performance.
4. Squeeze vendor margins to focus them on cost and value requirements, by using market testing, bids, re-sourcing and negotiation.
5. Build a thorough understanding of the cost drivers within the supply chains, of likely targets for cost down.
6. Develop a briefing pack for vendors, identifying the required way forward (for you and for them).
7. Visit vendors to brief them, and secure their commitment to the process.
8. Develop and provide training in value-analysis, target-costing and profit-planning techniques.

Category examples	Price down		Cost down		Cost out	
	Negotiation	Rationalization	Value engineering	Joint development	Target costing	Profit planning
Stationery	High	High	Low	Low	Low	Low
Castings	Medium	Low	Medium	Medium	Low	Low
Packaging	Medium	High	Full	Full	Full	Full
Computers	Full	High	Medium	Low	Full	Medium
Capital	Low	High	Medium	High	High	Medium
Consultancy	High	High	High	Low	Full	Full
Advertising	High	High	High	Low	High	Full
Own label goods	Medium	Low	High	Full	Full	Full
Key components	Low	Low	Full	Full	High	Full
Total product	Medium	Medium	High	High	Full	Full

Relevance: Low · Medium · High · Full

Figure A6.4 *Different categories of expenditure demand different approaches to drive down costs. Resources need to be allocated accordingly*

Appendix 7

Buyer remuneration in the UK

Companies in the UK have the benefit of an excellent independent guide to salaries and remuneration of professional buyers in the UK, namely the *Purcon Salary Study*, produced for many years by Purcon Ltd (www.purcon.co.uk), a company founded in 1978. At the time of writing, the latest biannual survey is available for only £150.00 (exc. VAT). The Study gives comprehensive details of the ranges of salary packages, bonuses and company car ownership of buyers in the UK, in line with:

- role seniority;
- company size;
- region of the UK;
- industrial sector;
- qualifications.

The following excerpt from the Summer 2007 Study is provided with kind permission from Purcon Ltd.

JOB LEVEL 5 (OF 7 JOB LEVELS)

Job description

- typically 7–12 years' functional experience;

- a team leader or manager with up to 30 staff, OR a senior developmental role with project responsibility, OR a management consultant;
- operates at a strategic level, actively contributes to and implements overall strategy and direction, but also maintains a significant operational element to their duties (50 per cent);
- annual spend typically up to £250m;
- typically no responsibilities outside of the procurement function.

Typical job titles

- purchasing manager
- supply chain manager.

ANALYSIS

Sample overview

Job level 5 roles represent around 17 per cent of the survey sample – but as with the previous survey, the sample size has continued to increase, providing a more accurate reflection of the actual changes taking place within the market.

Overall salary levels

The level 5 median salary has increased in line with the market in general with the media salary now standing at £67,556, indicating that the significant increase for the 12 months prior to the Winter 2006 survey was a result of the change in sample size and increased interval between surveys, rather than a reflection of changes in the market.

Qualification

Over 53 per cent of Level 5 roles have achieved CIPS qualification, but as was indicated in previous surveys, this does not appear to attract a premium in terms of base salary. At this level it would appear that salary and qualification are not particularly related, and it is likely that 'value' is placed on a combination of both skills and experience.

Company size

Level 5 salaries follow the established and well-known trend of increasing with size of company. At the market median, Level 5 roles in large companies earn £8,000 more than their counterparts in smaller organizations.

Regional analysis

As expected, with a median salary of over £70,000, London stands out as the highest paid region by a clear margin. This is followed by East Anglia and Scotland, although these results must be viewed with caution given the Level 5 sample size in these regions.

Industry analysis

At the market median, Level 5 roles receive the highest salaries within the Construction sector – £74,179. This is followed by Petrochemicals, which pays above £70,000 at the market median.

Bonuses

At Level 5, bonuses are a fairly common component of remuneration, received by 61.1 per cent of the sample. The median bonus received is 17.1 per cent of salary.

Company cars

A company car benefit is also a typical component of Level 5 remuneration, with over 70 per cent of roles receiving either a car or a cash alternative.

Base salary (£) by age

Age band	Lower quartile (LQ)	Average (median)	Upper quartile (UQ)	Average (mean)
20–25	–	–	–	–
26–30	61,389	62,676	64,901	61,418
31–35	55,998	61,617	74,860	64,887
36–40	56,499	67,199	81,989	69,326
41–50	59,830	65,087	77,056	67,859
51+	50,244	59,046	64,734	60,875
All ages	56,186	67,556	75,270	65,840

(I was curious about the reported decline in average base salaries above the age of 41, and asked Purcon's Mark Peasley for his views on the phenomenon. He attributed it to three factors, the first two related to the increased commercial emphasis on buying and supply chain efficiency, which has resulted in core changes in the market for buyers:

- The development of buying as a positive career choice. An increase in the number of professional qualifications, training and university courses has resulted in an increase in the quality and education of individuals entering the profession. This, combined with the increased understanding of buying within organizations and the competition for good candidates in the market, has led to rapid promotion for high-quality (internal and external) candidates, and fast-track career development schemes. As a consequence of this, the average age of the workforce at this level is reducing.
- Owing to their experience and knowledge in their specialist field, senior buying professionals have moved into positions that incorporate buying and supply chain responsibility as part of a wider role. As a result of their varied responsibilities outside of buying, they are no longer included in the Purcon Study purely for buying professionals.
- Older executives tend to be more risk-averse than younger ones, and therefore less willing to switch employers in order to land a superior package.)

Base salary (£) by company size

Number of employees	Lower quartile	Average (median)	Upper quartile	Average (mean)
Up to 250	51,441	57,487	64,456	60,645
251–2,000	52,396	61,799	69,156	65,596
Over 2,000	59,116	64,312	76,086	66,345

Base salary (£) and company car (% receiving) by region

Region	LQ	Median	UQ	Mean	Car
London	61,794	71,150	80,027	70,101	72.4%
South East	55,732	62,312	72,336	65,675	71.6%
Midlands	56,602	63,412	76,168	67,384	69.9%
South West	54,718	62,326	72,705	62,356	72.3%
North West	60,197	65,110	75,735	69,580	66.3%
East Anglia	51,773	69,754	82,737	66,455	54.3%
Scotland	–	67,062	–	72,732	49.6%
North East	53,053	60,998	70,885	61,261	82.1%

Base salary (£) and company car (% receiving) by sector

Sector	LQ	Median	UQ	Mean	Car
Aerospace and defence	52,837	67,804	77,328	66,002	52.3%
Automotive	54,831	63,769	77,072	65,931	88.6%
Construction	62,946	74,179	79,222	71,094	–
Electronics	56,237	63,071	71,663	62,116	83.6%
Engineering	50,716	61,618	74,955	62,952	68.5%
Finance	59,587	64,082	73,694	67,941	69.4%
FMCG	55,762	62,298	72,041	63,828	92.3%
IT	59,922	62,328	71,352	65,321	61.9%
Logistics	46,684	65,829	75,078	61,436	51.1%
Petrochemical	62,028	73,924	70,280	69,384	33.8%
Pharmaceutical	61,456	67,793	73,782	70,309	58.7%
Public sector	65,767	67,133	77,594		85.6%
Retail	60,443	63,057	76,319	64,636	63.1%
Services	58,514	64,928	77,483	66,320	66.8%

References

Brown, D and Wilson, S (2005) *The Black Book of Outsourcing: How to manage the changes, challenges, and opportunities*, John Wiley & Sons, New York

Corbett, M (2004) *The Outsourcing Revolution: Why it makes sense, and how to do it right*, Dearborn Trade Publishing, Chicago

Eakin, D and the BuyIT e-procurement Best Practice Network (2001) *BuyIT Online Auctions*, BuyIT, London

Her Majesty's Treasury, March 2007

Hughes, J, Ralf, M and Michels, B (1998) *Transform Your Supply Chain: Releasing value in business*, International Thomson Business Press, London

Kotler, P and Lee, N (2005) *Corporate Social Responsibility: Doing most good for your company and your cause*, John Wiley & Sons, Hoboken, NJ

Kraljic, P (1983), Purchasing must become supply management, *Harvard Business Review*, **61** (5), pp 109–117

Sheridan, D (1991) *Negotiating Commercial Contracts*, McGraw-Hill, London

Index